The time is now

31 DAYS FOR
ADVENT
FOR SMALL GROUP
OR PERSONAL USE

The time is
now

Amy Orr-Ewing

Contents

Introduction

Advent is upon us. Last year, on 1 December, my three children came bounding into my and my husband's bedroom at 5am, eagerly asking if it was at long last time to start their Advent calendars. My children had been anticipating the calendars, which are, in themselves, an aid to anticipating Christmas itself.

Advent is a time of preparation – a time when we reflect on the coming of the Lord in the Person of Christ. In these daily studies, together, we will dwell on God's preparation of people and events in history, which made the incarnation possible.

Throughout the month of December, as Christmas Day draws closer, Christians all over the world focus on the arrival of Jesus Christ in His first Advent, and reflect upon His return as King – the second Advent that is yet to come. Advent is a word which originates from the Latin and means 'coming' or 'arrival'. In the midst of this double focus on past and future, we reflect together on God's perfect timing. We look back into history and see the preparing work of God through the ages, how He involved ordinary individuals and their daily lives in the grand sweep of redemption history. In looking forward we see how God is preparing His people now in hope for Jesus' glorious return.

When we read the word 'time' in the New Testament, it is a translation of one of two Greek words – *chronos* or *kairos*. *Chronos*, from which we get our English word 'chronology', means the time on your wristwatch, time on the move, time passing from present to future, and so becoming past. *Kairos*, on the other hand, means 'the appointed time in the purpose of God', the time when God acts. For example, in Mark 1:15 we read that 'the time has come'; the *kairos* is fulfilled. *Kairos* is time in a qualitative rather than a quantitative sense. It is time as a stirring breakthrough, a significant occasion, an imminent, immeasurable quality. The New Testament writers use the word *kairos* to communicate the idea of God's time; it is eternal reality breaking into the now. When we read about *kairos* we sit up and listen.

When Jesus stepped into time to proclaim the kingdom of God among us, He came to show us in *chronos* the reality of *kairos*. 'Jesus took John and James and Peter up the mountain in ordinary, daily chronos,' writes L'Engle. 'Yet during the glory of the Transfiguration they were dwelling in kairos.'[1]

The Christian is given New Testament language to explain the tremendous encounters and life-shaping moments that occur in all our lives. Within unfolding day-to-day time (*chronos*), God intervenes and works out His purposes: 'I tell you, now is the time [*kairos*] of God's favour, now is the day of salvation' (2 Cor. 6:2).

On our Christian journey, the questions of guidance, discovering God's will and purpose for us now, and submitting to His timing, loom large as daily discipleship themes. Where should I live? Whom should I marry? What kind of work should I do? To which areas of service in my church should I commit? Who am I led to share the gospel with? These are all questions of purpose and timing, and questions about which God cares. In this season of Advent we will be pursuing God in His Word and through prayer, expecting Him to guide us personally in our lives and help us to grasp our calling in this generation. God's purpose can sometimes be hard to discern in the moment – it is often through looking back that we detect the purpose of God in circumstances.

Ravi Zacharias imagines God as the Grand Weaver who makes something beautiful from all the threads of our lives:

> Now if an ordinary weaver can take a collection of coloured threads and create a garment to beautify the face, is it not possible that the Grand Weaver has a design in mind for you, a design that will adorn you as he uses your life to fashion you for his purpose, using all the threads within his reach? Once you begin to see God's hand in your life, you will know that his workmanship within you and through you was tailor-made, just for you. His design for your life pulls together

every thread of your existence into a magnificent work of art. Every thread matters and has a specific purpose.'[2]

In these Advent studies, we will together do precisely that – look back and see how perfectly the timing of God works out in the lives of individuals who could not have grasped the big picture of which they were a part. And as well as looking back we will also look forward, embracing hope for the future and regaining a biblical perspective on the time we have.

How to Use

This Advent book is designed to be read day by day through December alongside the Bible. Each day includes a suggested Scripture reading and then some reflection upon God's Word. There is also a suggestion for personal reflection and a prayer each day, and then a few questions to answer, under the heading 'Consider'. It may help to write down your answers to the questions in a notebook or journal, or you may want to discuss them with a friend or partner who is also following this study for Advent. At the end of each seven-day period there is a group activity, designed to bring together for weekly discussion people who may all be following the Advent readings individually day by day. You may want to take one of the sets of questions from the previous week and answer them together before carrying out the suggested group activity.

Let me encourage you to pray each day before you read Scripture and ask the Lord by His Holy Spirit to speak to you and open His Word to you in a fresh way.

Everyday Lives; Eternal Significance

1 Dec

Bible readings: Genesis 1:26-28; 3:1-6,14-15

Today, at the beginning of December, we reflect on the beginning of everything. Time itself began as God created the universe, the planets, the stars and us.

The word *geneseos* from which we get 'Genesis' means 'beginnings', and at the beginning of life on earth we encounter the first woman, Eve. Having famously been tempted and having plunged the world into a nightmare of consequences with her husband Adam, Eve hears from God that she will also play a part in redeeming the world. She is told that her seed will destroy the devil and his power. We read: '... I will put enmity between you [the serpent] and the woman, and between your offspring and hers; he will crush your head, and you will strike his heel' (Gen. 3:15).

The coming of Christ – the One born of a woman,

who would destroy the power and work of the evil one – had been prophesied right at the beginning of the Old Testament.

God's work of preparation begins in His perfect timing. Just as everything seemed to be collapsing in total failure, God's perfect creation spoiled by the first people to enjoy it, He reveals a plan of rescue and restoration. The season of Advent is a time of reflection on Jesus coming into the world, and we reflect on how God has been doing His work of preparation in hearts throughout history, making things ready for the incarnation of Christ. Both men and women were caught up in the story of preparation – many never knew in their lifetime the significance of the role they were playing in salvation history, but their participation is a powerful witness to the truth that God uses ordinary people like you and me in His extraordinary redemptive plans for the world. And that even in times of terrible darkness and sorrow, failure and unbelief, God can be at work in us, bringing something wonderful to pass. Stuck in the here and now as she was, Eve could not have known precisely what her role would be in the line of the Messiah, but as the recipient of this prophecy and the mother of the human race, she played an important part. As time unfolded, God would intervene and weave together His plan of salvation.

Yet we are so impatient – we want promises to be fulfilled right away and find it hard to wait through unfolding time for the breakthrough *kairos* moment. This is more obviously true when we are younger – we long impatiently for the presents of Christmas Day and our birthdays. As we get older this impatience can be equally desperate but more discreetly hidden – wanting to see answers to our prayers for the healing or salvation of family members, wanting a new job, wanting to get married or have a child, wanting our debts to be finally paid off. God sees all the longings of our hearts and our desperation for the waiting to be over, but sometimes He is speaking to us in the time of waiting. Will we hold on to Him in unfolding time? Will we persevere until that *kairos* moment? Are we willing to trust Him even if, like Eve, we never live to see the fulfillment of what we have hoped for?

Pause to reflect:

Perhaps something in your church, a personal difficulty or a recent news item has made you despair. Don't pretend that things are better than they are but, in the midst of the darkness now, can you hold on to the truth of Jesus' light and love? As you remember the promise to Eve that her seed would crush the serpent's head, allow faith in Jesus to rise in your heart.

In prayer now be realistic about the darkness, disappointment, failures and sorrows you face today – and over all of these pray for the light of Christ to dawn.

Pray:

You are Christ, my Holy Father, my Tender God, my Great King, my Good Shepherd, my Only Master, my Best Helper, my Most Beautiful and my Beloved, my Living Bread, my Priest Forever, my Leader to my Country, my True Light, my Holy Sweetness, my Straight Way, my Excellent Wisdom, my Pure Simplicity, my Peaceful Harmony, my Entire Protection, my Good Portion, my Everlasting Salvation.

St Augustine (AD 354–430)

Consider:

1. Describe how you feel when you have to wait for an answer to prayer.
2. Look back on your Christian life and see how God has worked even through difficulties and times of waiting to bring about something good.
3. Think of a *kairos* moment in your Christian life. Thank God for what He did.

2 Dec

Bible reading: Genesis 4:1-2,25-26

It is exhilarating to be involved in naming a child. When I discovered I was pregnant with twins, my husband and I spent many hours dreaming up names. We did not know whether we would have two girls, two boys, or a girl and a boy, and so we came up with three sets of names. It was not until the actual birth of each boy that we could give them the names we had talked of endlessly. We had waited a long time and gone through years of sorrow before being able to have the boys. I remember the hospital room vividly as I held first one and then the other – it was a true *kairos* moment for us and we were suddenly sure that each name was right for each boy.

In verse 1 of this passage we read that Eve named her firstborn Cain. No matter how excited about first pregnancies we are today, it can be as nothing compared to the excitement of Eve – hers was the first ever pregnancy. She didn't know what was going to happen – she just watched it unfold with amazed eyes. The child was born in a manner no human being could have predicted. We have books about birth and pregnancy now but, however much you read about it in advance, the experience of birth – whether holding the mother's hand or labouring yourself – is utterly overwhelming. Eve didn't know how any of it would happen or even how many months she would have to wait. She was full of hope – none of us could ever cherish higher hopes for a child than Eve. When her son was born we are told she named him Cain, which means 'brought forth'. She goes on to say, 'With the help of the LORD I have brought forth a man' (v.1). The Hebrew literally means 'I have brought forth the man even Jehovah'.

Of what does this remind you? Remember yesterday we read the famous promise of Genesis 3:15, when God said, '… [the seed of the woman] will crush [the serpent's] head'? God did not specify which woman and when this might happen. It must have been the deepest hope of Eve, who was responsible for the Fall, that she might be the one to bear the Messiah who would crush the serpent. Eve, the one to whom the promise had been spoken, must have wondered as she gave birth to Cain, 'Could this child be the One?' She was full of hope. We don't know how long this hope persisted, how long it took for her dreams to be shattered, but we do know that by the time the second child was born she named him Abel. Abel means 'meaninglessness' or 'vanity' – it is the word that the writer of Ecclesiastes uses all the time. This strongly suggests that by the time Abel was born, Eve had seen enough in Cain's life to bring her disillusionment, and change her hope to pessimism or even despair.

How ironic that the one Eve thought was going to be Messiah became a murderer and the one she named 'meaningless' and 'vanity' was the very one, 2,000 years later, Christ would call 'righteous Abel' (Matt. 23:35). As Luke's Gospel tells us, it would be through Eve's third son, Seth, that the line of the Messiah would be established. Even in these early chapters of Genesis, we are being pointed towards Jesus – the time coming when God Himself would enter into the world and destroy the serpent and his works.

Pause to reflect:

For Eve, the immediacy of the promise of redemption filled her heart with hope, but she also experienced real despair when things didn't unfold as she had expected. With the gift of hindsight we can look back through the Bible and see God's unfolding purpose and plan. We can see that the Messiah did come – in the Person of Christ, as the seed of another woman, Eve's seed, Mary. How often do we jump to the conclusion that God has forgotten us, or not kept His word, when we do not yet see the full picture? In this Advent season reflect on the unfolding purpose and plan of God in bringing His Son into the world and how this might speak into the situation in which you now find yourself.

Pray:

Use the words of the Litany of St James – held by many to have been written by James the brother of Jesus. If you can, say or sing these words aloud:

Let all mortal flesh keep silence,
and with fear and trembling stand;
ponder nothing earthly-minded,
for with blessing in His hand,
Christ our God to earth descendeth,
our full homage to demand.

King of kings, yet born of Mary,
as of old on earth He stood,
Lord of lords, in human vesture,
in the body and the blood;
He will give to all the faithful
His own self for heavenly food.

Rank on rank the host of heaven
spreads its vanguard on the way,
as the Light of light descendeth
from the realms of endless day,
that the powers of hell may vanish
as the darkness clears away.

At His feet the six-winged seraph,
cherubim, with sleepless eye,
veil their faces to the presence,
as with ceaseless voice they cry:
Alleluia, Alleluia,
Alleluia, Lord Most High!

Consider:

1. Think about any situations in your life in which you need to stand back and trust God's timing and will.
2. Have there been times in your life when God has used unexpected people or circumstances to answer your prayers? What can you learn from this?
3. What does it mean to you that Jesus was prepared to come into the world as a human being?

3 Dec

Bible readings: Genesis 18:1-2,9-15; 21:1-3; 22:1-2,9-14

In today's readings we encounter Sarah, Abraham and Isaac. As time (*chronos*) unfolds God is continuing to work in history towards the fulfilment of His promise of salvation. Abraham is called by God to found the nation through whom every nation would be blessed, but he and his beloved wife, Sarah, are unable to have children. The *kairos* event never seems to happen – how could this promise of a nation of descendants be fulfilled without even one child? Time continues to pass – in fact, so much time passes that Sarah is really elderly when God gives the promise of a son to Abraham and she overhears it. Sarah laughs out loud at the prospect of conception and birth – surely too much time has gone by. It is a miracle then that a year later she is able to give birth to a boy and give him a name which means 'laughter' – Isaac. God had fulfilled His promise after all and against all odds.

Horrifying then that when the child is a young man he is asked to carry the wood up a hill for his own sacrifice. Poignantly, Abraham is asked to give his son, his only, beloved son as an offering on an altar. After all they have been through, Abraham, Sarah and Isaac are required to make the ultimate sacrifice – the laying down of the life of their most longed for, precious son. But the *kairos* moment happens – God's audible voice intervenes, shattering the inevitable, and Isaac is spared. God provides a ram for the sacrifice. In His perfect timing God underscores both the cost and the *source* of redemption – the cost is everything, the life of a beloved only son, but the One paying will be God Himself. This story is known as the *aqedah*, which means 'the binding' of Isaac. This word emphasises Isaac's willing coalescence with the sacrifice, since Abraham was a very elderly man and Isaac was strong enough to carry wood up a mountain. If he had wanted to resist he could have fought his way out of the situation. The love of God the Father and God the Son are both foreshadowed in this amazing story of redemption.

At Advent we look back in history at the 'how' of the fulfilment of this promise: Jesus, God's one and only beloved Son, is born into the world. The ultimate *kairos* event, is the incarnation of God as a human being in the Person of Christ. But the imagery of a sacrificial lamb is still here – Jesus is born in a stable where sheep lived, and the first humans to hear of His birth, after Mary and Joseph themselves, were shepherds.

In John's Gospel Jesus is called 'the Lamb of God'. Jesus is the perfect, spotless, pure One. This lamb is the Lamb 'of God'. This is a genitive and could mean 'provided by' God or 'belonging to' God – probably both. This Lamb is the *aqedah* Lamb of Genesis 22:8 – the ram provided by God. Abraham had been told to take his only son Isaac and offer him to God. This was a picture of what God was going to do Himself – He as the Father was to give His beloved Son Jesus for our sake. For Abraham, God intervened and provided the animal for the sacrifice so that his only son was spared. Hundreds of years later, Jesus, God's own Son, is born into the world, in order to be that sacrifice once and for all. He carries His own wooden cross up a mountain but, this time, there is no voice from heaven sparing Him – Jesus is the Lamb who is sacrificed for us to free us from our sin.

Pause to reflect:

In God's perfect timing Abraham and Sarah had a son who was to foreshadow His own Son. They must have given up hope so many times, yet God delivered them even in the darkest hour. Meditate on what the incarnation cost God and how much that means He loves you.

Pray:

> Mine are riches, from Thy poverty
> From Thine innocence, eternity
> Mine, forgiveness by Thy death for me
> Child of sorrow for my joy[3]

With the words of this famous carol in mind, spend some time thanking Jesus for coming into this world and being the long promised 'Lamb of God'. Seek His forgiveness and cleansing power in your life, being as specific as you can.

Consider:

1. What does it mean to you personally to have to wait for things for which you are praying?
2. Have you ever laughed at a promise of God?
3. Do you think it significant that Isaac was a willing adult in this story?

4 Dec

Bible reading: Genesis 45:3-11

God's timing is of the utmost importance in the Bible. This is
something we rarely think or speak about in the Western Church,
where, just as in the culture around us, we want the things we want
instantaneously. We are used to getting what we want even when
we can't afford it, and just going into debt if necessary. We have lost
the capacity to watch and wait. All the advertising geared at us and
our children, especially in the run-up to Christmas present buying,
exacerbates this. Yet Advent is the polar opposite of immediate
consumption fuelled by debt. The run-up to the birth of Christ begins
at the creation of the world – all of history as it unfolds in time
(*chronos*) is in a cycle of preparation for this *kairos* event, God coming
into the world. But there are multiple *kairos* episodes during this time
of preparation: life stories recorded for us in the Bible, through which
we see that God is making us ready for the coming of His Son.

The life of Joseph is described at greater length than that of any
other character in Genesis, and the fullness of detail all seems to
point to *Christ*. The incarnation of God's Son is not just prophesied
in the Old Testament, it is also prefigured and prophesied in people's
very lives, as we saw with Isaac, so that Jesus' life and message
would be recognisable when He came.

Joseph is the beloved son of his father, who is sent away from
home on an errand. In the course of carrying out this errand, he is
sold for pieces of silver, and he becomes a servant. He is tempted by
a seduction, but comes through untouched by impurity. He is then
shackled and imprisoned unjustly, he suffers and, through that suffering
and his faithfulness, he becomes a saviour to a starving world. The
very life of Joseph is punctuated by *kairos* moments, all of which point
forward to Christ. Although he couldn't have known it, each step along
the path of his life had specific purpose in the mind of God.

Pause to reflect:

Joseph was caught up in the process of preparation for the coming of Jesus into the world. Even with his own vindication and success, Joseph could never have known in his lifetime the significance of the role he was playing in salvation history, preserving the line into which the Messiah would be born and prefiguring and prophesying the Person of Christ. But Joseph's participation in salvation's story is also a powerful witness to the truth that God uses ordinary people like you and me in His extraordinary redemptive plan for the world.

Pray:

Dear Lord Jesus, thank You for coming into the world in order to make God known to us. Thank You for humbling Yourself so much that men and women of old were caught up in Your coming to save us. Thank You for spending time with ordinary people and reminding me today that whoever I am and whatever my inadequacies, You can use me for Your kingdom and glory's sake. Please help me to serve You and make You known on earth today and every day that I am alive. For Your name's sake. Amen.

Consider:

1. Are there people in your life for whom you are the main point of contact with the Christian faith? What might that mean for you?
2. Are you aware of God's timing in placing you in particular places at particular times? Might there be people He is sending you to speak to and to serve?

5 Dec

Bible reading: Joshua 2:1-2,8-11,17-18

Today we encounter another significant woman who was to feature in the genealogy of Jesus. This lady is called Rahab and she lived in Jericho during the era of Joshua. As we reflect on the coming of Christ into the world during this Advent season, we see that unexpected people get caught up in the story of grace. How could Rahab, a Gentile woman and a prostitute in the city of Jericho, have possibly imagined that she would be included in God's plan to redeem the world? We see that she believed in the Lord – '... for the LORD your God is God in heaven above and on the earth below' (Josh. 2:11) – but the significance of this personal faith for those of us living thousands of years later could not have even occurred to her. Living in her own time (*chronos*) her actions of faith and obedience are part of a *kairos* moment.

Rahab makes an agreement that when her city is destroyed, all who take shelter in her house (presumably through believing her message and warning) will be saved, and that her house, which was in the city wall of Jericho, would be marked out by a scarlet cord, so that no soldier would be confused that those within were to be spared. Imagine the scene, then, when Joshua and his army march around the city of Jericho for six days and on the seventh day they march around it seven times. The walls collapse, but Rahab's house is spared, it must have been the only bit of the wall of Jericho left standing. What an astonishing picture of grace – through a scarlet red cord symbolising her faith and trust, this woman and all who listen to her are spared.

It is powerful and prophetic that Rahab ends up in the genealogy of Jesus – her son is Boaz, who goes on to marry Ruth (we'll read more about her tomorrow). Even in Jericho God was at work in His perfect timing, preparing the world for the coming of His Son. This tells us as future generations something profound about the nature of His love for the world – no one is beyond the remit of His mercy, not even a prostitute from an enemy country. Anyone who will believe and trust will be welcomed into the family of God through the coming of His Son into the world.

Pause to reflect:

Do you ever feel completely insignificant – watching the days and years roll by, wondering if God has any great purpose for your life? Remember that He used the simple faith and trust of an outsider like Rahab in her own era in a way that is still significant today.

Pray:

Ask the Lord to help you to follow Him and grow as a disciple in time now, but with eternal priorities front and centre in all that you do – that You will be able to sow seeds that will take root and last beyond the here and now.

Consider:

1. Why do you think God included this Gentile woman Rahab in His Son's line?
2. Are there any people in your life whom you have written off as disinterested in God or beyond redemption? Why? How might you begin to think and act differently towards them?
3. Can you think of a time when you had to trust God and step out in faith as Rahab did? What happened?

6 Dec

Bible reading: Ruth 1:19-2:13

'In the days when the Judges ruled' (Ruth 1:1) refers to an era of unprecedented challenge to faith in the one true God. Israel had come through years of upheaval, from slavery in Egypt to the Exodus, wandering in the wilderness to the conquest of the land. And now they were in the land, struggling to settle whilst facing significant economic, moral and social pressures. It is into the darkness of these questions that the book of Ruth shines, telling the story of ordinary people facing ordinary events. The inclusion of this story in the Bible tells us that the lives of ordinary men and women are not insignificant to God. He knows us in all the detail of our lives – He cares for us and numbers the hairs on our heads.

The book of Ruth introduces us to two key characters: Naomi and Ruth. Naomi leaves Bethlehem during a famine at the instigation of her husband Elimelech. When Elimelech and Naomi's two sons die, she is left far from home with a foreign daughter-in-law, Ruth, who chooses to go back with Naomi to her homeland. But when Naomi arrives, people barely recognise her, asking, 'Is this Naomi?' Her reply 'Don't call me Naomi … Call me Mara, because the Almighty has made my life very bitter' (v.20), is poignant, as Naomi means 'pleasant', Mara means 'bitter'. When Naomi uses the word 'Almighty' here it is *Shaddai*; she refers us to God as 'cosmic ruler'. Naomi places her suffering in the context of God's sovereignty, but she renounces her own identity. She is so completely at the end of herself that she asks to be called Mara, but God doesn't give up on her.

When bad things happen we are psychologically and spiritually affected – our ability to think rightly about God, others and ourselves is skewed. This story is descriptive of such a situation. But God does not leave Naomi in this desperate state – she is delivered. However, her dark night of the soul goes deep, and it is not skirted over.

Maybe you can identify with that utter despair and blackness; it is amazing that this reality is included in the preparation of God for the birth of His own Son. At Advent we are encouraged to remember both the darkness and the light – the darkness of the world into which Christ comes and the blazing light of Jesus Christ. As we shall see, Ruth has a significant role in the genealogy of Jesus. In the midst of the darkness and difficulty we are shown the God who never lets go of us.

Naomi directs Ruth to the harvest field and ultimately to a man called Boaz, who notices Ruth because she has worked so hard without taking a rest. Ruth asked, 'Why have I found such favour in your eyes that you notice me – a foreigner' (2:10). But Boaz commends her: this is not an issue of race – Ruth has been faithful and committed. Boaz goes on to speak of her as now included in the covenant, as someone who has taken refuge under the Lord's wings (v.12). This language of the covenant recognises Ruth as being defined by whom she has taken refuge in – in Yahweh, under His wings. It is God's plan that in His perfect timing this woman Ruth – a foreigner – would be included in salvation's story.

Naomi begins to ponder a plan that Boaz could take care of Ruth via the provision of a tradition called levirate marriage. This meant that if a widow was left childless, a male relative of her late husband could marry her and give her a son, but the son would take the name of the first husband. Could this be God's providence? Would a man be prepared to father a child in these circumstances?

In the context of a strong belief in God's providence, Naomi makes the plan. Naomi is proactive. She encourages Ruth to go right over and propose to Boaz. There was another, closer relative who would have fitted the bill but remains unnamed. However, Naomi believed that Boaz was the man for Ruth. It may seem radical today for a woman to propose to a man, but in this culture it was truly astonishing. Ruth was to get into the bed of this man after he had eaten and drunk during the harvest party time, and trust in his righteousness, trust he would not take advantage of her. This takes real courage. But Ruth does it. She trusts – she trusts Naomi, she trusts Boaz and, ultimately, she trusts God.

Pause to reflect:

God is faithful! Reflect on times in your life when you have trusted Him and He has proved faithful. As you remember His faithfulness, take some time to thank Him for specifics. God's timing is perfect, even out of the darkness of famine, bereavement and poverty, He made a way for something beautiful to happen. And He chose these humble individuals – Naomi and Ruth – to play a significant role in preparation for His coming into the world.

Pray:

Take some time to pray in your own words, thanking God for His faithfulness and asking for His help as you trust Him each day.

Consider:

1. Why do you think God chose a foreigner like Ruth to be in the line of His Son?
2. Have you ever had to trust God in difficult circumstances? What was that like? Did you experience God's faithfulness to you?

7 Dec

Bible reading: Ruth 4:1-16

Continuing from yesterday the story of Ruth, we see here that Boaz takes care of the details of the proposed marriage at the city gate. This was the place for business and legal matters to run the course of due process. It is so fascinating that this story of providence and love is rooted in the material world where reason, legislation and process are honoured. The Bible does not take us out of the real world – we are called to read it and live out the call of God on our lives in the public square; not in some private 'religious' sphere, but in real space, time and history. These *kairos* events happen in *chronos* time, reminding us that we too, who live ordinary lives in the real world can be caught up in the redemptive purposes of God's kingdom here on earth.

Boaz buys Elimelech's field, making it clear that he plans to raise up sons for him through his marriage to Ruth. The man who takes on this kind of levirate marriage is known as the 'kinsman redeemer'. This is prophetic of what Christ does for us – coming into the world in the incarnation as one of us and then redeeming us and covering us with His blood.

Boaz and Ruth are married and we are told that God granted that she conceive a child. Again the providence of God is clear here. Out of all of this struggle, bereavement, famine, poverty, shame, loneliness and loss, Ruth is finally able to have a son. Ruth conceives. Life is affirmed in a culture surrounded by the darkness of death and destruction, something which has many resonances with us today.

Naomi, who was Mara, is now Naomi again. The baby's life changes bitterness into joy. What a beautiful picture of grace. And as if to underscore the significance of grace here, through this son Ruth becomes an ancestor of King David and ultimately of Christ. This Gentile woman demonstrates in her life that inclusion in the people of

God is by faith, that God rewards faithfulness in relationship to Him and that we all need to be redeemed and covered. Her story is prophetic – not only does she physically point to Christ, she also demonstrates in her life something of what Jesus was to come into the world to do.

Pause to reflect:

Think about how your life can point to Jesus as the Redeemer. Ask the Lord to fill you with the Holy Spirit and empower you to live for Him in a way that shows people through your actions as well as your words how great He is.

Pray:

Thank You, Father God, for the redemption through Jesus that we enjoy. Thank You for using an ordinary person like Ruth – an outsider who had lost everything – to be a part of Your plan for the world. I pray for my family members and friends who do not yet know You – naming them before You today *[take some time to be specific]* – and I ask You to be at work in their lives, making Yourself known. Help me to be faithful in speaking of You and pointing to You with my life. In Jesus' name. Amen.

Consider:

1. Does anything about you point the people around you to the bigger story of Jesus and His forgiveness?
2. Are there pockets of bitterness in your life? Can you ask God to help you to forgive and let go of these?

Group Activity:

Hand out two pieces of paper to each person in the group. Say the Lord's Prayer together. When it comes to the line 'forgive us our sins', take a moment of quiet to each write on one of the pieces of paper the things for which you are asking God's forgiveness. Then gather the papers in a large saucepan, light a match and let the papers burn. If you have an open fireplace, burn the papers there. As you say the line 'as we forgive those who sin against us', take your second piece of paper and write down the names of those you need to forgive. Ask for God's help to forgive these people, and again gather the papers and burn them. Then continue saying the rest of the Lord's Prayer together.

Foretold Long Ago

8 Dec

Bible reading: Psalm 2:1-12

A series of prophecies about the coming of Christ as the 'Messiah'
(Anointed One) arise during the reign of King David over Israel.
In these prophecies the kingly and godlike qualities of the coming
Christ are revealed. The Lord promises David through the lips of
a prophet called Nathan that He will bring into being an eternal
kingdom for His Son through one of David's own descendants:
'… I will establish his throne for ever. I will be his father, and he will
be my son' (1 Chron. 17:12–13).

   Have you ever been chosen out of the blue for something
wonderful? When he was five years old, one of my sons won the
main prize at a chocolate party. It was an enormous chocolate bear
and he shared it with the whole family for weeks. A year later he
still talked about that win wistfully. Being chosen for something can
be wonderful, but it can also bring huge responsibility. David was

identified and then anointed as a future king by the prophet Samuel during the reign of Saul. God was working within time to establish His Son's line, and He chose David to be a king and prophet and, as such, David points beyond himself to the higher King and Prophet who was to be born – Christ.

David was the youngest of the large family of boys belonging to Jesse (Boaz's grandson). Despite being the youngest and smallest, David, the most unlikely candidate from Jesse's sons, was chosen. But he was not able to take the throne immediately. A long road of difficulties and persecutions lay before him. Through various temptations and tests it was only his trust in God that kept him alive. During this season of suffering, David would pour out his grief to God in inspired psalms, and this worshipful writing continued after Saul's death when David was crowned and he became the most outstanding king ever to rule Israel.

In the course of his life, through the hardships and the triumphs, David used the poetic gift he had been given and frequently prophesied the coming Messiah: 'Why do the nations conspire and the peoples plot in vain? The kings of the earth take their stand and the rulers gather together against the LORD and against his Anointed One' (Psa. 2:1–2). This prophecy alludes to the attempt by Herod to destroy the newborn Messiah with the killing of the innocents that he commands after the visit of the Magi. But the psalm goes on: 'He said to me, "You are my Son; today I have become your Father [or begotten you]"' (v.7). God's own Son will be born in time and, as David warns, this Messiah, this Son will be the judge of all: 'Kiss the Son, lest he be angry and you be destroyed in your way, for his wrath can flare up in a moment. Blessed are all who take refuge in him' (v.12).

In this psalm the truth is revealed that the Messiah is the Son of God. David writes more about the perfection and divinity of the Messiah in several subsequent psalms. For example, in Psalm 45, David speaks of the coming Messiah: 'Your throne, O God, will last for ever and ever; a sceptre of justice will be the sceptre of your kingdom. You love righteousness and hate wickedness; therefore God, your God, has set you above your companions by anointing you with the oil of joy' (vv.6–7). Jesus was going to be born as a man in space, time and history – but He is also God. The coming Messiah would be God with us.

Pause to reflect:

This season of Advent is a time of preparing our own hearts for the coming of the Lord, and we do this by reflecting on God's preparing work in history. Long before Jesus came in history, God was working within time, working in the hearts of people and through events to make the incarnation possible. Reflect on how you are being prepared for serving God through the season of Advent.

Pray:

Use the words of St Francis of Assisi (1181/1182–1226):

Prayer of Self-giving

I beg You, Lord,
let the fiery, gentle power
of Your love
take possession of my soul,
and snatch it away
from everything under heaven,
that I may die
for love of Your love
as You saw fit to die
for love of mine.

Consider:

1. Why is it important that Jesus' coming was prophesied hundreds of years earlier?
2. Have you grasped the wonder of the truth that Jesus is God and that David prophesied that God would one day come into the world as a man? How do you feel when you hear Jesus demeaned and His name used as a swear word in our culture? Why do people use His name in this way – what does it say about the situation we live in today?
3. What does it mean to take refuge in God in your own Christian life?

9 Dec

Bible readings: Matthew 22:41-45; Psalm 110:1

Do you sometimes wish that instead of remembering the coming of Christ into the world we could point to the physical, material Person today and say to people, 'Look, here is Jesus'? We may feel that if only we had that physical proof, everyone would believe. Somehow we are living in the wrong time – if we were in a different age everything would be so different. Yet even the Christmas story teaches us otherwise. We see that when Herod and his advisors heard of the star and consulted their research, they knew that the King would be born in Bethlehem, but they do not go with the Magi to worship. Instead Herod, knowing the truth, instigates his own search for the child in an attempt to kill Him, destroying many other baby boys in the process.

Even in the midst of the miracles Jesus performed during His public ministry, the Pharisees challenged His status. They knew that Jesus was powerful and righteous, yet they tried to catch Him out. So Jesus

Himself asked them a question using one of the messianic prophecies of the Psalms in order to expose their hypocrisy and His own divine status. He says: 'What do you think about the Christ? Whose son is he?' They reply with the obvious answer: 'The son of David.' And Jesus goes on, 'How is it then that David, speaking by the Spirit, calls him "Lord"?' (Matt. 22:41–43). Jesus quotes from Psalm 110 to underscore His point. How can the Messiah who is David's descendant be His 'Lord' unless He is divine? The response to this is silence …

Even Jesus faced unbelief and opposition to His divinity.

Pause to reflect:

During this Advent season, as we reflect on the Light coming into a dark world, it can be easy to wish we lived in a different, easier time, when things were clearer or easier for people to believe and respond to. But did such an easy time ever exist? God has placed us on the earth now for a purpose – He has called you and me to live now and to follow Him now. He came into the world in the Person of Christ; He went to the cross to redeem us. All of this was prophesied in times long ago. His kingdom has been established – the time is now to make Him known.

Pray:

Lord, in the turmoil and darkness of our world I cry out to You – the Light of the World. I recognise that I can do nothing and You can do all things. Help me to live for You today. Help me to be a light pointing to You. I want to rest in Your mercy and truth today. Please fill me with the Holy Spirit. Open my eyes to see Your hand at work in my life and in the lives of those around me and help me to have the courage to stand, speak, give and behave in a way that honours You. In Jesus' name. Amen.

Consider:

1. Do you have friends who ask for more proof of who Jesus is? How can you keep on praying for them and witnessing to them?
2. How do you cope with opposition to Christ and Christians? How can we be grace–filled and confident in the face of opposition?

10 Dec

Bible reading: Isaiah 9:1-7

Today's reading is a familiar Advent piece. The promise arises in the 'gloom' and 'distress' so familiar to 'the people walking in darkness'. The messianic prophecy begins with a promise that Galilee will feature heavily in the light-filled redemptive purposes of God. Such geographically accurate prophecy written hundreds of years before Jesus lived and ministered so extensively in Galilee should not be lost on us.

The prophetic words given to Isaiah spoke of the light for all the Gentiles, for all the nations of the globe, all ethnic groups. 'The people walking in darkness have seen a great light' (v.2). We walk in physical darkness: and into the darkness of the night the star showed the way to the stable where Jesus was born and the angels made the sky aflame just as Jesus brought light to the world. We walk in spiritual darkness: many live without the knowledge of the spiritual freedom we find in Jesus – in bondage to the occult, and the sins and grief of past years bind many into destructive tendencies. This is the darkness that leads to abuse in families on religious grounds, or violence in the name of religion. This is darkness and can only be named as such once we have seen the light. We walk in moral darkness: lives are extinguished without a second thought. Jesus was born into this kind of darkness and He brought His light to bear upon it. Herod wanted to kill the young and innocent when Jesus was born, but he was unable to thwart God's plans. We walk in intellectual darkness: the Scriptures say our minds are darkened; they are switched off to what is good for us. And just as when someone switches on the light in a darkened room it takes time for our eyes to adjust to the light, so we need our minds to be renewed when we come to know Him. Jesus was born into a dark world and brought light with perfect teaching that has never been rivalled.

There is political darkness: some people live in dark and hidden regimes, where neighbours spy on one another, where there is no freedom – Jesus brings hope into such a darkened life, and brings a temporality to it. That darkness will not last forever. Jesus was born into such a darkness and brought light. He was born into a young family that had been uprooted by a census to pay taxes, and in the midst of this the joy of a new birth was brought to this poor family. There is also death's darkness: the darkness which haunts every human heart – the moment every heart stops beating, when we leave those we love, and have no more time to put things right. Death stalks every heart until another light can overcome it. It is this darkness that Jesus' death and resurrection overcomes.

As the prophet Isaiah wrote, 'The people walking in darkness have seen a great light'.

Pause to reflect:
Remember the darkness from which Jesus as Messiah has come to rescue us. Ask Him to shine His light and truth upon your life.

Pray:
Lord Jesus Christ, You are the true Light that has come into the world. I praise You that You are mighty to save. I thank You that You are the One who delivers us from darkness. I surrender to You today.

I cry to You to shine Your blazing light into all the areas of darkness in my own life. *[Take time to bring before the Lord your fears, sins, hurts, difficulties, broken relationships.]* I thank You that You are my Deliverer. I pray that the people I love *[take time to name unbelievers for whom you are praying]* may come to know Your deliverance personally in the power of the Holy Spirit. In Your holy name. Amen.

Consider:

1. Do you think 'the people walking in darkness' is a description to which our culture can relate? What are the sources of gloom and distress around you?
2. How can you be involved in making the light of Christ known locally where you live?
3. Can you think of areas of darkness in your own life that have been transformed by the light of Christ? Thank Him for His work in your life.

11 Dec

Bible reading: Isaiah 11:1-10

I sometimes feel for Isaiah. He was called to be a prophet before all the exciting aspects of the 'good news' had been fully revealed in the life, death and resurrection of Jesus. So, like many prophets of the Old Testament, he begins on what might sound like a depressing note. Isaiah's ministry started in a difficult time, when Judah was rather like a tree stump that had been cut down. But even in the midst of that darkness and confusion he was given the incredible role of explaining something fundamental about the gospel that would come to fruition hundreds of years later. Something profound will happen – out of the stump of Jesse a shoot will come up and from that root, a branch will bear fruit.

Isaiah goes on to give definition to this hope – this shoot, root, branch will be a Person upon whom the Spirit of the Lord will rest. A Person will be born in history who will be full of wisdom and understanding, perfect counsel and the might of God, knowledge and the fear of the Lord. This Person who will be born in the line of David and Jesse will also be a Judge who is perfectly righteous and faithful. Knowing nothing of the Person of Christ, Isaiah perfectly describes the coming of the Lord Jesus. This is a *kairos* moment.

Then the prophet goes on to describe something even further in the future – and this time we identify more with Isaiah because we have not yet seen this either. We look back on the first coming of Christ into the world at Advent, but we also look forward to His second coming. In his prophecy Isaiah tells us a little of what it will mean: 'The wolf will live with the lamb, the leopard will lie down with the goat, the calf and the lion and the yearling together; and a little child will lead them (Isa. 11:6).

When Jesus returns He will make all things new. We will be safe from all that once sought to hurt us: 'They will neither harm nor destroy on all my holy mountain ...' (v.9). There will be no death, destruction or pain. It is hard to imagine such a life, but it is as real as the truth of Jesus' first coming. We can look back and see that Isaiah's prophecies of the Messiah were fulfilled in Jesus' first coming; what a brilliant foundation for us to look forward as we wait for the rest of his prophecy to be fulfilled.

Pause to reflect:

Advent is traditionally a time for Christians to think about the second coming of Christ. Take some time to remember that this will be as real as Jesus' first coming and that, like Isaiah, we look forward to it.

Pray:

Dear Father, I thank You for Your invitation to come close to You. I thank You that You made this possible by giving us Your Son, Jesus Christ. I thank You that You do not leave us languishing in our brokenness, shame and rebellion, but You make a way for us and call us home. Please speak to me this week through Your Word. Challenge my habits, thoughts and inclinations. Help me to live in the light of Jesus' return. Through Jesus Christ. Amen.

Consider:

1. Do you think much about the second coming of Christ? How does the truth of Christ's imminent return shape your decision-making?
2. Do you feel ready for Christ's return or are there things you want to do before that day? List these things and lay them before God, asking Him to shape your days and transform your priorities in the coming year.

12 Dec

Bible reading: Isaiah 42:1-9

One of the unique features of the Messiah in this first Servant Song of Isaiah is the gentle and peaceful manner in which He goes about His task of restoration. In a world in which violence and aggression rule the roost, where earthly conquerors proclaimed their victory over the weak with pomp and visual displays of supremacy in the street – the Messiah would come quietly and in humility. Think of the contemporary displays of earthly power we see on our television screens – the military paraphernalia that is paraded when a statement is necessary. Even the architecture of our global cities shouts out the status and power of the nations to which they belong. Isaiah prophesied, in a time of Babylonian imperial power, that when the Messiah comes, He will not echo the displays of power we are used to.

This famous passage is electrifying on so many levels in what it says about the promised Messiah. In our Advent study today we focus on verse 3: 'A bruised reed he will not break, and a smouldering wick he will not snuff out. In faithfulness he will bring forth justice …' I had not really thought about what this might mean until I came across the explanations offered by the theologian Kenneth Bailey, who lived in the Middle East for sixty years. Reeds in the Middle East are not what we in Britain might think of: thin stems used for flower arranging. Reeds are huge towering structural plants used for the construction of things such as houses and boats. They can carry great weight, unless of course the reed is bruised, in which case it is utterly useless – in fact, it would be dangerous if used and so, out of concern for others, a bruised reed would be broken up and put in the fire so that no one could mistake it for something useful.

The Messiah, by refusing to break the bruised reed, would be an astonishing Person. The Messiah would take and redeem lives that were utterly broken and useless, good for nothing but destruction. This is underscored by the other image used by Isaiah: the Messiah would not snuff out a smouldering wick. In houses made of reeds there was a high risk of fire. That meant that under every oil lamp a pan of water waited so that when a wick was burned up and finished, instead of falling onto the floor, it fell through the lamp into water. This is a smouldering wick, a completely useless and used-up wick. The Messiah would not snuff out such a wick.

Pause to reflect:

Long before he knew what Jesus would be like, Isaiah was called to prophesy and point forward to this unique Messiah who was to come.

In his own time, yet pointing forward, Isaiah was inspired by the Holy Spirit to make Jesus known. In our time now we look back on the fulfilment of this prophecy in the Person of Christ – but do we live it out? Do we demonstrate in our time the compassion and powerful purpose of Christ in taking utterly broken and devastated lives and seeing His powerful love and transformation redeeming the brutalised?

Pray:

Take some time to ask the Lord to fill you with compassion for the broken world we live in. Be open to Him speaking to you about specific situations and leading you to act compassionately in His name.

Consider:

1. Have you ever heard the term 'compassion fatigue'? Do you think Christians are susceptible to becoming weary of doing good? Do you detect this in your own life?
2. Have you ever been on the receiving end of compassion or kindness from another person when you were hanging on by a thread? Thank God for that person and ask Him to help you to be involved with others in the same way.
3. Are there people you know whom you have written off as beyond the scope of redemption? What do you need to do about this?

13 Dec

Bible reading: Daniel 7:13-14

Are you the kind of person who asks a lot of questions? It is apparently a sign of great intelligence to ask the right questions.

There is a well-known anecdote of an unnamed rabbi who always asked questions. And he often responded to others' questions with a question of his own. When he was asked by one of his students, 'Rabbi, why do you always answer a question with a question?' he replied: 'Why shouldn't I answer a question with a question?'

In John's Gospel Jesus asks over thirty questions. All of them are profound, but today we will be thinking about one in particular. It comes in John 9 after Jesus has healed a man who had been born blind. After the healing there is some controversy amongst the religious leaders from the Temple, and the man comes back to see Jesus again. Jesus asks him the question: 'Do you believe in the Son of Man?' (v.35). If you have ever read one of the Narnia stories by C.S. Lewis, perhaps Aslan's names for human beings will come back to you here – men are 'Sons of Adam' and women are 'Daughters of Eve'. Is Jesus here asking, 'Do you believe I am a human being?' At Advent that would be a good question to reflect on – it is marvellous and wonderful that in Christ, God came to earth as a man. But that is not what this question means. Jesus is referring to a prophecy in the Old Testament. A vision was given to the prophet Daniel – in God's perfect timing He was revealing something profound about His coming Son hundreds of years before Jesus was born.

Daniel has this vision of 'one like a son of man coming with the clouds of heaven'. He 'approached the Ancient of Days' – this is a name for Yahweh, denoting His eternity and authority. It is extraordinary then that this Son of Man can approach Him without crawling on hands and knees. The Son of Man has 'authority, glory and sovereign power' – He is divine and He has authority for judgment. We are told that 'nations and men of every language worshipped him' – He is not a tribal deity but the universal God; 'His dominion is an everlasting dominion'. This is not for one culture or a particular period of time, His kingdom is eternal and will never be destroyed.

Here's the question Jesus asks the man and, as we walk through the season of Advent, He asks us too: 'Do you believe in the Son of Man?' Do you believe in Jesus in the way described? Do you really believe that He is God, that He has authority and glory and power, that He will judge all people, that He is the God of the universe, for all people groups, that He is everlasting?

Pause to reflect:

Think about what it means that Jesus Christ is the Son of Man. Are you willing to surrender to Christ in your day-to-day life, worshipping Him as Lord of all? What does it look like practically today to answer Jesus' question as the man did?

> 'Who is he, sir?' the man asked. 'Tell me so that I may believe in him.' Jesus said, 'You have now seen him; in fact, he is the one speaking with you.'
> Then the man said, 'Lord, I believe,' and he worshipped him.
>
> John 9:35–38

Pray:

Use the words of this famous hymn as a prayer, changing 'him' and 'his' to 'you' and 'your' …

> All to Jesus I surrender
> All to Him I freely give
> I will ever love and trust Him
> In His presence daily live.

I surrender all,
I surrender all.
All to Thee, my blessed Saviour
I surrender all.

Judson W. Van DeVenter (1855–1939)

Consider:

1. Jesus is to be worshipped by people of every culture, language and ethnicity. How can this truth shape your church's mission?
2. Do you find your own belief in Christ as the only way to God, shaken in our pluralistic society? Can you echo the man in John's Gospel, 'Lord I believe'?

14 Dec

Bible reading: Micah 5:2-4

There are few things as harmful to a relationship as a string of empty promises never fulfilled. But we see from today's reading that God doesn't believe in empty promises. The prophet Micah had received a prophecy of hope against the backdrop of humiliation. Micah was writing in the context of a city under siege in 701 BC. He prophesies that Bethlehem, the town of David, will be important again – God will raise up a Messiah from that place.

Hope would rise from the place that Israel's most beloved king, King David, had come from: Bethlehem. 'Bethlehem Ephrathah' means 'a house of bread', promising fruitfulness, not starvation in the future, a longed-for end to the famine of siege. Micah's is a vision of hope and of a delivering king, while things are incredibly bleak all around.

God is encouraging His people, and the little town of Bethlehem in particular, to hold on in the difficulties of the time they are in and to wait for the *kairos* event – for the Deliverer from Bethlehem to arise.

Micah's prophecy is that hope would take the shape of a ruler. The title here is not 'king' but 'sovereign' or 'ruler'. There will be something different about the new Ruler, and yet He will have royal blood in His veins, from the tribe and the place of Bethlehem. This is a clear messianic prophecy, which Jesus wonderfully fulfils. Micah could hardly have imagined how significant his words would be.

We also see that the Ruler will be as a shepherd to people: 'He will stand and shepherd his flock in the strength of the LORD, in the majesty of the name of the LORD his God' (v.4). This is a hope for care and nurture. In the midst of the loneliness and sorrow of a siege, the prophet looks forward to the time when the Messiah will come and shepherd the people. How wonderful that Jesus called Himself 'the Good Shepherd' and fulfilled this prophecy so completely.

The prophecy of Micah also tells us that the turning point (or *kairos* event) will be a baby being born: 'Therefore Israel will be abandoned until the time when she who is in labour gives birth …' (v.3).

Even though this prophecy had been given around 701 BC, in a time of desperation for Israel after 700 years – the time comes and *hope is fulfilled*.

Pause to reflect:

Don't give up when times are tough – God doesn't believe in empty promises. There were so many reasons for God's people to despair, so many reasons to believe that things would never get better. After 699 years the Jews could have concluded, 'God has let us down, things will never change', but they would have been wrong. God fulfilled Micah's prophecy, and Jesus, this baby born in Bethlehem, was all that they had been waiting for. In Trafalgar Square every year there is a Christmas tree which is given by Norway as a thank you to the British people for helping liberate them during the Second World War. They waited under oppression, and eventually the promise was fulfilled. As a sign of their gratitude they faithfully send a tree to London each Christmas. They remember what was achieved. They remember to say thank you.

Pray:

Thank God for sending Jesus in His perfect timing and ask Him to help you to trust His timing in your life.

Consider:

1. Do you find it difficult to wait for answers to prayer? What have you been praying for for a long time?
2. Have you been let down by other human beings who have failed to deliver on their promises to you? Have you allowed this to shape your perception of God and other people?
3. Have you thanked God for what He has done in your life recently? How could you get into a habit of thankfulness in your Christian life?

Group activity:

Each write a list of answers to prayer. Write another list of things you are still praying for that have not yet been given to you. Find two large envelopes and write on one 'Please' and on the other 'Thank You'. Put all the answered prayer lists in the 'Thank You' envelope and ask each member of the group to share one answered prayer. Put all the lists of things you are still praying for in the 'Please' envelope and ask each member of the group to share one prayer need. Spend time in prayer for one another, thanking God for His faithfulness in the past and lifting your needs to Him.

The Time Came ...

15 Dec

Bible reading: Luke 1:5-20

During this Advent season we are exploring the unfolding purposes of God within time. As we come into the New Testament (literally New Covenant) we see that 'the fullness of time' has come. The new is now here. We have seen individuals being prepared for the coming of the Messiah, God's Son, and now, at the beginning of Luke's Gospel, we see the story begins in the Temple. A couple called Elizabeth and Zechariah are elderly and childless. 'Both of them were upright in the sight of God' – the barrenness was a deep sorrow but not a punishment. Zechariah was a priest and he had been chosen by lot as the one individual who could walk into the holy place of the Temple to burn incense. Whilst in there an angel appears and speaks: 'Do not be afraid, Zechariah; your prayer has been heard. Your wife Elizabeth will bear you a son, and you are to give him the name John' (v.13).

We learn from this that Zechariah has been praying for a son.

But his reaction is rather surprising. He is a priest, he is a righteous man, he has prayed for years and a glorious angel appears to him. But his reaction is: 'How can I be sure of this?' (v.18). Being told by a messenger of God that it's going to happen isn't enough for him; doubt and even cynicism had entered his heart. The disappointment of years of unanswered prayer had rendered him low on faith.

The angel's response appears to be rather harsh – Zechariah, whose job it is to lead worship and teach the people, will be unable to speak until the birth of the child. Is this a little inconsistent with the angel's reaction to Mary? She too encountered an angel, but the message she received was unexpected – it was not something she had prayed for. She asks: *'How* will this be?' (Luke 1:34, my emphasis). She's merely asking for clarification on how, being a virgin, she's going to become pregnant. Mary's question, unlike Zechariah's, expresses no doubt of the truth of what the messenger is saying.

God's timing for Zechariah and Elizabeth to have a son was something they couldn't see and, in the midst of their sorrow at their childlessness, Zechariah was overcome by doubt and cynicism. This is not as unusual in a minister as we might hope. The disappointment might be to do with health struggles, perhaps, but cynicism in the heart of a Christian is a dangerous thing.

Pause to reflect:
Are there things I have given up waiting and praying for?

Pray:
Dear Lord, help me to leave my cynicism and weariness at the foot of Your cross. Forgive me for giving up when I have been disappointed. Please fill me with Your Holy Spirit and cause hope to rise again in my heart for the things of Your kingdom in this Advent season. In Jesus' precious name. Amen.

Consider:

1. Do you identify at all with Zechariah and his loss of hope?
2. Looking back over your Christian life, what good has come out of waiting and persevering?
3. How might you be able to encourage other Christians and leaders in your church who may be struggling with cynicism?

16 Dec

Bible reading: Luke 1:23-25,39-45

The Hebrew form of the name Elizabeth means 'worshipper of God'. Everything that we know about Elizabeth, wife of Zechariah and mother of John the Baptist, is to be found in the book of Luke. She was a descendant of the priestly line of Aaron, and a close relative of the Virgin Mary. Luke tells us that Elizabeth had lived a blameless life with her husband in one of the hill towns of Judea. But she had reached old age with her prayers for a son unanswered.

As we learned yesterday, Elizabeth's husband Zechariah was burning incense in the Temple when the angel Gabriel appeared to him and announced that a son who would be 'great in the sight of the Lord' (Luke 1:15) would be born to Elizabeth. When she was already six months' pregnant, the angel appeared to Mary to tell her of the birth of Christ. Mary came to visit Elizabeth, and when Mary entered the house the baby in Elizabeth's womb leaped for joy. We read that the elderly lady Elizabeth was filled with the Holy Spirit and 'In a loud voice she exclaimed: "Blessed are you among women, and blessed is the child you will bear!"' (vv.41–42).

As if this were not dramatic enough, Elizabeth goes on to call Mary the 'mother of my Lord' (v.43). Elizabeth was not the kind of person to whom exciting things happened. Yet here she is in old age, expecting a miraculous son and now recognising with prophetic power the unborn incarnate Christ in Mary's womb and choosing to worship Him. Having waited her entire life for something good to happen, she does not stay on the sidelines and observe – she enters into the action wholeheartedly. In the fullness of God's timing she has a significant role to play. She is the mother of John the Baptist and she is able to follow him in worshipping Christ.

We get a strong sense that Elizabeth has learned from Zechariah's situation in what she says next: 'Blessed is she who has believed that what the Lord has said to her will be accomplished!' (v.45). Elizabeth is able to commend Mary for her faith.

At Elizabeth's delivery, her friends and neighbours rejoice with her and, when the child is brought for circumcision, they want to call him after his father Zechariah, but Elizabeth says, 'No! He is to be called John' (v.60). Again she is faithful to the promise the angel had given her husband. She has seen the consequences of cynicism and is determined to be full of faith and hope.

Pause to reflect:

Elizabeth must have felt forgotten by God after years of faithful service, with time (*chronos*) passing year after year. Yet when God's marvellous intervention came in His perfect timing, this woman met the *kairos* events with joy and faith. She had not become hardened by disappointment; somehow she had learned to trust God even in lengthy difficult times. This was all a part of God preparing her to be a part of the Advent story. She gives birth to the forerunner of Christ, John the Baptist.

Pray:

Take some time to pray using the line of the Lord's Prayer: 'Your kingdom come.' Ask for His marvellous intervention in your life and in the life of your church.

Consider:

1. Have you ever felt forgotten by God? What does Elizabeth's story say to you about this?
2. How can you be more open to the work of the Holy Spirit in your life?
3. What breakthroughs are you praying for in your own life and in the life of your church for the coming year?

17 Dec

Bible reading: Luke 1:67–80

After John the Baptist was born, Zechariah wrote on a tablet: 'His name is John' (Luke 1:63). Straight away he was able to speak again and he was filled with the Holy Spirit and prophesied. The words of that prophecy are all the more powerful because of the passing of time (*chronos*). Zechariah had nine months of silence to meditate on God's Word, both in the Old Testament and through the angel. While his silence was enforced as a punishment for unbelief, God was able to turn all things to good. Did Zechariah in the silence of those months when he was unable to talk with his wife or friends, begin to realise the significance of the days in which he was living? I know in my own life that the spiritual disciplines of silence and solitude, though rarely practised, help me to stand back and grasp the wonders of God and the *kairos* events He initiates in the midst of the craziness and busyness of daily life.

Zechariah emerges from the months of silence filled with the Holy Spirit, and he sings what has come to be known as The Benedictus. The majority of this song is taken up not with his own son, John the Baptist, whose birth is cause enough for wonder and worship, but with the salvation that the coming Messiah is going to bring. Only two verses (vv.76–77) refer to John the Baptist specifically: '… you will go before the Lord to prepare the way for him, to give his people the knowledge of salvation through the forgiveness of their sins …' All of the other verses of The Benedictus are about the significance of the coming of Jesus.

Zechariah is a changed man. He begins in verse 68: 'Praise be to the Lord, the God of Israel, because he has come and has redeemed his people.' When we first met him, this priest Zechariah could not believe that his prayer had been answered – even when a blazing angel appeared to him and spoke a promise that his wife would have a child. Now Zechariah is filled with the Holy Spirit and is so confident of God's redeeming work in the coming Messiah that he speaks about it in the past tense. With conviction and faith, a promised act of God is for Zechariah as good as done. In contrast with his cynicism and doubt he is now utterly confident.

Zechariah speaks about the Messiah as 'a horn of salvation'. He is not referring to a musical instrument, but to the deadly horn used as a weapon by the wild ox. This is the only place in the New Testament where Jesus is called a horn, so we have to go back to the Old Testament, as Zechariah would have, to know what this means. In Psalm 92:9–10, for example, a horn is a sign of strength and a means of victory. Jesus is the horn of salvation because He is a deadly weapon and tremendous power which, according to Zechariah in verse 71, God will use to save His people from their enemies and all who hate them. The Messiah will one day literally destroy His enemies and gather His people into His land and rule them in peace. We look forward to this during the Advent season when we reflect on the second coming of Christ. But this raising up of a horn of salvation also means that the redeemed are rescued 'from the hand of our enemies' so as to 'serve him without fear in holiness and righteousness before him all our days' (vv.74–75). God's aim in raising a horn of salvation is to create a holy and righteous people who live without fear because they trust Him. This is the heart of Zechariah's song and of Christmas – this is what Jesus comes to do.

Pause to reflect:

Can you carve out an hour or two in the next couple of days to be silent and reflect on the wonder of the incarnation? Ask God to fill you with His Holy Spirit so that in the midst of the unfolding time (*chronos*) in your life you might grasp the *kairos* truth of Jesus' coming.

Pray:

Thank You, Jesus, that You came into this world as a man. I praise You that, in Paul's words in Philippians 2, You who, being in very nature God, did not consider equality with God something to be grasped, but made Yourself nothing, taking the very nature of a servant, being made in human likeness. And being found in appearance as a man, You humbled Yourself and became obedient to death – even death on a cross! Therefore God exalted You to the highest place and gave You the name that is above every name, that at the name of Jesus every knee should bow, in heaven and on earth and under the earth, and every tongue confess that Jesus Christ is Lord, to the glory of God the Father. Amen.

Consider:

1. As we get ready for Christmas in this Advent season, remember that the One who came as a baby in Bethlehem is also the victorious Deliverer. What does this mean to you?
2. What does it mean to live in the light of the second coming of Christ? Does this make a difference to your priorities and decision-making?

18 Dec

Bible readings: Luke 1:80; 3:1-6

Elizabeth and Zechariah's son grows strong and goes out to live in the wilderness where 'the word of God came to [him]' (Luke 3:2). As we have seen, a succession of ordinary people have faithfully lived before the Lord in their time, scarcely knowing the significance of the role they were playing in the future arrival of the Messiah, God's Son. And now we come to John the Baptist – the very forerunner of Christ. He fulfils Isaiah's prophecy of a voice calling in the wilderness and preparing a way for the Lord.

John prepares the way for Jesus to come by preaching a message of radical repentance 'for the forgiveness of sins' (v.3). John's ministry opens the hearts of his hearers to their need for forgiveness. He doesn't preach only with words, he also baptises people, powerfully illustrating the truth of the human need for total cleansing, washing by complete immersion in water.

John does not seek admiration or power – he always points to Jesus. When asked if he is the long expected Messiah he is clear: 'I baptise you with water. But one more powerful than I will come, the thongs of whose sandals I am not worthy to untie. He will baptise you with the Holy Spirit and with fire' (v.16). He understands the time in which he lives and the purpose for which he has been born

– his purpose is to point to Jesus and usher in the kingdom of God in the ministry of the Messiah. It is very rare to meet someone this secure in his or her own calling and identity. How tempting it is to secretly wish for the role, impact, status or gifts of another person. But to envy a fellow Christian, even wanting good things that God has given them, is to be unhealthy and immature as a follower of Christ. We deny His work in us here and now, we insult Him by deriding the calling and gifts with which He has entrusted us.

Pause to reflect:

Am I pointing to Jesus with my words and with my life? Have I received His love and His calling on my life, accepting this without envying others who appear to be more important or successful?

Pray:

John Wesley (1703–1792) wrote a prayer which people said together once a year, committing themselves to real discipleship. Pray this today, if you dare:

I am no longer my own, but yours.
Put me to what you will,
Rank me with whom you will;
Put me to doing, put me to suffering;
Let me be employed for you or laid aside for you,
Exalted for you or brought low for you;
Let me be full, let me be empty;
Let me have all things, let me have nothing;
I freely and wholeheartedly yield all things to your pleasure and disposal.
And now, glorious and blessed God, Father, Son and Holy Spirit,
You are mine and I am yours. So be it.
And the covenant now made on earth, let it be ratified in heaven.
Amen.

Consider:

1. Do you take credit for successes in your life and ministry or do you point to Jesus?
2. Do you draw security from your usefulness to God or are you able to be 'laid aside' for Christ?
3. Are there people around you whom you envy? How can you turn away from this?

19 Dec

Bible reading: Luke 2:25-35

Simeon was a godly man who lived through the occupation of his land and, with other people of prayer, waited quietly and patiently on God, hoping for the salvation the Messiah would one day bring. Joseph and Mary brought the infant Jesus to Jerusalem when He was forty days old, so as to make a sacrifice as required by the Law of Moses (Lev. 12:1–8).

The details in this story are utterly fascinating – many scholars believe that Luke spent significant time researching his Gospel with Mary the mother of Jesus, so we know, for example, that Mary and Joseph were relatively poor, as they could not afford to offer a lamb (Luke 2:24).

As the story unfolds we are given an amazing insight into God's timing. As this poor couple come into the Temple, they meet an old man named Simeon, a man who has spent his life in prayer, worship and faithful expectation of the day when God would comfort His people. God had promised Simeon through the Holy Spirit that he would not die without seeing with his own eyes the Messiah, the anointed King.

We do not know whether he knew of the details of Jesus' birth

– the star, the stable, the angels and the Magi – perhaps through the testimony of the shepherds or from someone else. But, in God's perfect timing, the *kairos* moment occurs – led by the Holy Spirit he is in the right place at the right time in order to meet the holy family in the Temple. There is no equivocation or doubt in Simeon's mind – this is the *kairos* moment of his life, he has longed for the fulfilment of the promise of the Messiah and he sees in the child Jesus the focus of his hopes and longings.

Simeon takes the child in his arms. As a mother myself I remember feeling uneasy about people wanting to hold my babies in the early days, unless they were close family members or friends. How must Mary have felt as this elderly man took her baby? But He was no ordinary child, and Mary knew that truth. Perhaps she anticipated the prophet's recognition of divinity in her child. Simeon breaks into praise – a song later known as the 'Song of Simeon' or the Nunc Dimittis (Latin, 'now dismiss').

In the baby Jesus, Simeon recognised that the Messiah had come and, with the fulfillment of the hope of his life, he was now ready 'to depart this life in peace'. This is extraordinary. In that *kairos* moment Simeon is so happy that he is ready to die. What has he seen in this child Jesus?

In Jesus, Simeon saw immediately that salvation had come.

'For my eyes have seen your salvation …' (v.30). Simeon recognised Jesus as the One who would bring salvation to humanity. In a culture that revered age and learning, this is utterly revolutionary: an old man pays homage to a baby and calls Him God's Saviour for the world.

In Jesus, Simeon saw that the prophecies of the Old Testament were being fulfilled: '… you have prepared in the sight of all the people …' (v.31). The Old Testament was known by the nations of the world around Israel – people knew of their hopes and expectations of a Messiah. Simeon here declares that the time has come for the fulfilment of those promises, and this is a certainty, so people will know for sure that the Messiah has come. The time they had been longing for was here. Imagine his excitement after the long expectation – the time is now!

In Jesus, Simeon saw that the light for the Gentiles had come. He recognised in that moment that Jesus was not only a Saviour for Israel but for the whole world: '... a light for revelation to the Gentiles ...' (v.32).

Here Simeon grasps something profound about Jesus that even the disciples struggled to realise. In that *kairos* moment of revelation, as he holds the Son of God in his arms he sees the truth. Simeon also saw in Jesus that this child was 'for glory to your people Israel' (v.32).

Pause to reflect:

Think about the eternal significance of this *kairos* moment in Simeon's life. He is holding the Son of God in his arms and he is able to recognise who Jesus really is. In the light of that truth he is totally surrendered to God. He is able to die in peace, seeing the fulfilment of his hopes.

Pray:

Thank God for His perfect timing – that Simeon got to hold the baby Jesus and that Jesus is a light to the whole world. Spend time thanking the Lord for His glorious revelation of Himself in Jesus.

Consider:

1. What might Mary and Joseph have felt in the moment of encounter with Simeon?
2. What is the dream of your life? Is there a fulfilment of a dream that might cause you to echo with Simeon the Nunc Dimittis?
3. Have you really grasped the truth that Jesus is the light to all the

nations? Are there people in your life whom you have thought are somehow too far away for Jesus' light to be relevant to them?

20 Dec

Bible reading: Luke 2:36-40

Yesterday we met the prophet Simeon, an old man who had waited a long time in hope for the coming of the Messiah. Today we encounter the prophetess Anna, who was in a similar position. She was an elderly lady widowed after seven years of marriage. We meet her at the age of eighty-four. She had dedicated her adult life to worshipping 'night and day, fasting and praying' (v.37). We are told that she 'never left the temple' (v.37). She was a woman of extraordinary self-denial and commitment. She must have experienced genuine hardship – emotional and material – in her life, and yet she was completely committed to the Lord.

We are told exactly who Anna is – we know her father's name (Phanuel) her tribe (Asher – one of the northern tribes) and her age. This shows us that timing is important to God. This is no random encounter. Anna is a real person who lived in history, and she got to witness the breaking into history of the eternal God in the Person of Christ.

She approaches Mary and Joseph after Simeon has prophesied. We read that Mary and Joseph are overwhelmed by what they have heard: 'The child's father and mother marvelled at what was said …' (v.33). Simeon goes on to bless Mary and to warn her that 'a sword will pierce your own soul too' (v.35), prophesying the sacrificial death of Christ. It is into this extraordinary *kairos* moment that Anna steps. She immediately begins to pray. She gives thanks to God and she quickly tells everyone around her about Jesus. No doubt the people

who hear her know who she is – she would have built a good
reputation after all those years in the Temple. And here she was,
introducing Jesus – speaking of Him as Messiah to all those who
hoped for redemption.

Anna receives a wonderful reward for her faithful service – she
gets to see the Messiah with her own eyes. She also gets the honour
of being one of the first evangelists recorded in the Gospels.

Pause to reflect:

Throughout her years of praying and fasting, in the sorrow of her
widowhood, could Anna have realised the significance of her life?
She had no children – could she have known that future generations
(including us) would know her name and remember her? With
hindsight this all seems obvious but, in her tragic circumstances,
Anna would not have seen this. Yet she got a front row seat for the
redemption of the world. God rewarded her years of faithfulness.

Pray:

Thank You, Lord, that You care for individuals. Thank You that
we know Anna's name today and that this is a sign to me that my
name is written on Your hand (Isa. 49:16). Thank You that You
honoured the faithfulness of Your servant Anna and that You are
faithful in my life too. Thank You that the redemption Anna foresaw
and proclaimed was realised in Jesus' life and that I can know this
personally. Amen.

Consider:

1. What do you think of Anna's commitment to seeking God? Do
   you ever fast and pray?
2. Anna was a widow and, because of her loss, was not able to

have her own children. However, God brought good out of her painful circumstances. Are there any examples in your own life of suffering or disappointment out of which God has brought something good?

21 Dec

Bible reading: Luke 1:26-38

In our reading today we encounter the majestic angel Gabriel. He had already visited the priest Zechariah in the Temple to announce the coming of the baby John the Baptist. Now Gabriel comes to 'a virgin pledged to be married to a man named Joseph … The virgin's name was Mary' (v.27). Mary was a young teenager who had never slept with a man and whose family had chosen a husband for her.

Unlike Zechariah, Mary had not been praying for a baby, and certainly not for a virgin conception! Before she discovers what is on the agenda for this meeting, she is already troubled by the angel's greeting: 'You … are highly favoured! The Lord is with you!' (v.28). The fact that this greeting from the mouth of a majestic angel disturbed Mary, tells us that she is humble. She does not think of herself as the kind of person whom the Lord God of Israel would 'be with'. Maybe this is partly because she is a woman – she might have expected spiritually significant encounters to happen to other people, usually men.

The angel sees that Mary is frightened – he must be used to this reaction from humans! So, he encourages her again telling her that she has 'found favour' with God. The message he then goes on to deliver is astonishing. Mary's *kairos* moment has come – the intervention of God in human history, towards which all the Old Testament has been building, has arrived. The time is now.

Mary is told, *you* will be the one who has this child. The promise to Eve is finally to be fulfilled – the seed of the woman will crush the serpent's head. And Mary is the particular woman who will bring forth this seed. We realise that it is wonderful for her to meet Gabriel, but it must have been amazing for Gabriel to meet Mary, after all he knew of the prophecies. The New Testament tells us that the angels long to look into these things (1 Pet. 1:12). Gabriel was meeting the woman who had been chosen by God to bring forth the promised seed – God's own Son.

Mary will be with child – she will have a pregnancy that will run its course, she will then give birth to a boy, and at this point she is to give Him the name 'Jesus'. Even in the angel's message, the progression of time is honoured; she is taken through each step of this miracle.

Gabriel then goes on to describe Jesus: He will be called the Son of the Most High (v.32). This could not be clearer – Jesus is God. He will be given the throne of David. This could not be clearer – He will be the Messiah; the long awaited 'anointed one' who has been promised throughout the Scriptures. He will reign forever. This could not be clearer – the Messiah is not a king for a particular time, a military leader who will re-establish Israel as an earthly power, He is the divine eternal Ruler who can never be overthrown.

Mary's reaction to this marvellous theological revelation – the Messiah is God Himself and will be born in history in order to complete His eternal work of redemption – is to ask 'how' it will happen. She does not doubt that it will happen or that it can happen but, as she is going to be involved, she would like to know 'how'. Mary understands biology, she knows she is a virgin. The angel answers her, letting her know that the Holy Spirit will come upon her. This will be a miracle, a divine work. He reminds her that miracles are really possible, after all, her relative Elizabeth, who is elderly, is to have a baby. Nothing is impossible with God.

Mary responds with the famous words: 'I am the Lord's servant … May it be to me as you have said' (v.38).

Pause to reflect:

Meditate on Mary's response: 'I am the Lord's servant. May it be to me as you have said.' Reflect on her humility and willingness to participate in God's plan. Think about the truth that nothing is impossible with God.

Pray:

'May it be to me as you have said.' Thank You, Father, for Mary's faithfulness and willingness to be the mother of Jesus. Thank You for her example to us of Christian obedience. Help me to be faithful to You in every arena of my life – intellectual, vocational, with my resources, my body and my whole heart. I am Your servant, Lord. For Jesus' sake. Amen.

Consider:

1. 'Nothing is impossible with God.' Are there things you believe are impossible for Him to do?
2. Mary was asked by the Lord to be the mother of Jesus. What is the Lord asking you to do? Seek His guidance in your life. Are there dreams and visions He has placed in your heart already? Ask Him to help you fulfil His call on your life.

Group activity:

Choose somebody with an accurate watch to be timekeeper, then get into groups of four or five to pray.

In each group, one person sits in the middle, and the others stand around. Spend a minute in silence, listening to God for the person sitting. Then, for the next ten minutes, those standing pray for the person sitting, and share any words, Bible verses or pictures they have received. When the ten minutes is up, the timekeeper stops everybody and, in each group, a new person sits in the middle. Repeat the one minute of silence and the ten minutes of prayer until everybody has been prayed for.

If possible, have somebody make notes of the words, pictures etc for each person.

The Time is Now

22 Dec

Bible reading: Luke 1:46-56

Have you ever found yourself completely overwhelmed with the awesomeness of God and spontaneously prayed out of an overflowing heart? I remember doing this when a friend I had prayed for for two years to have a baby let me know that she was pregnant. The context of our passage today is that Mary has gone to visit her elderly relative Elizabeth. In a culture where women's worth was closely tied up with their ability to produce children, Elizabeth had lived a long life without being able to conceive. She was now six months pregnant and Mary, who knew the whole story, was visiting her. When Elizabeth's unborn child leaps with joy and Elizabeth herself calls Mary's unborn child 'my Lord' (Luke 1:43), Mary is overwhelmed. She is amazed by the miracle in Elizabeth's life, amazed by the greeting she has received and humbled to be encouraged in and commended for her part in the promise of God.

Mary begins like the psalmist: 'My soul glorifies the Lord and my spirit rejoices in God my Saviour' (v.46). She is completely taken up in worship; 'lost in wonder, love and praise', as Charles Wesley put it. She has had a *kairos* moment of revelation – the penny has dropped and she has realised in her deepest consciousness the wonder of what the Lord is doing. The result is overflowing praise. Have you ever known that sense of eye-widening revelation when a truth about God has just sunk in? This is a work of the Holy Spirit – it isn't something we can work up in ourselves. Christians throughout the ages speak of this kind of praise welling up inside them.

Out of the overflow of her heart Mary worships, and the reality of what is happening in her life at that moment in time forms the basis of her praise. She realises that although her pregnancy is happening then and there, she will be known by all future generations, because 'the Mighty One has done great things for me' (v.49). Mary knows that Jesus' coming into the world is not a personal truth just for her, but that Jesus' birth will have international and intergenerational significance.

Mary draws out a contrast between 'the proud', with whom she groups rulers on their thrones, and 'the humble'. Mary lived in a country under the occupation of a tyrannical empire. She knew what arrogance and hostility looked like and, in the midst of that sorrow, she remembers that God has sent His Son. She recognises that this is God's mercy in action.

Mary reflects on the wonder of God's actions in the past and the longings of previous generations who had looked forward to this moment, realising that God has 'remembered' to be merciful and that everything that is happening to her is a fulfilment of promises made to 'our fathers' (v.55). Mary's Magnificat is one of the most famous pieces of Christian theology ever to be written.

Pause to reflect:

Ask the Lord to restore wonder to you in your Christian faith. Turn away from taking for granted what God has done through the Person of Jesus.

Pray:

Almighty and everlasting God,
who stooped to raise fallen humanity
through the child-bearing of blessed Mary;
grant that we, who have seen your glory
  revealed in our human nature
and your love made perfect in our weakness,
may daily be renewed in your image
and conformed to the pattern of your Son
Jesus Christ our Lord.[4]

Consider:

1. Is Jesus truly 'Lord' of your life? Is He in charge? Elizabeth and the unborn John the Baptist recognised the lordship of Christ – do you?
2. Have you grasped the wonder of what God has done in sending Jesus? Have you known praise welling up in your heart in response to revelation?
3. Who are 'the proud' and who are 'the humble' today?

23 Dec

Bible reading: Matthew 1:18-25

Today we reflect on the Christmas story from the man's perspective –
we see how Joseph reacted to the news that Mary was going to have
a baby, and how God directly intervened.

Mary and Joseph were real people who lived in real time in
the real world. And, like a normal man who has discovered his
betrothed is pregnant when he knows that he has not slept with
her, Joseph assumes the worst. The Bible is not a mythical book or
a dream world where strange things happen and people think them
completely normal. Like Mary, Joseph understands biology and he
does the kindest thing he can think of – he decides to break off
the relationship quietly before the marriage. Matthew calls Joseph a
'righteous man' in this course of action. But imagine how Mary must
have felt. She too lived in real time in the real world.

But then a *kairos* event takes place. The time for God's dramatic
intervention has come, and Joseph has a dream in which an angel of
the Lord appears to him. It is only after this miraculous experience
that Joseph believes that Mary's Son is the Messiah. The angel is
explicit with Joseph: '... what is conceived in her is from the Holy
Spirit' (v.20). But it is not only Mary who has been selected for a
significant role – Joseph too has been chosen to play a major part in
redemption's story. His time has come. Joseph is told, '... you are to
give him the name Jesus ...' Resonant of Adam in Genesis 1, who was
given the role of naming that which God had made, now that God
Himself is entering into His creation as a man, Joseph is given the
awesome task of naming Him. His name will describe what He has
come to do. He is to be called Jesus 'because he will save his people
from their sins' (v.21).

Matthew reminds us that these are new events, but are also the
fulfilment of prophecies given much earlier in time. Isaiah had spoken

700 years earlier, and now what he had prophesied was coming to pass. All the anticipation, hope and waiting were over, the time had come. 'Immanuel – God with us' was now a reality.

Pause to reflect:

Jesus' arrival in the world meant that God was with His people. This happened in history, but it is true for all believers in all times. As Jesus Himself promises believers at the end of this same Gospel: '... I am with you always, to the very end of the age.' Allow that truth to sink in today. Established in history, Immanuel, God with us, continues to the present day and into the future.

Pray:

Immanuel, God with us, I worship You today

Immanuel, God with us, I recognise Your coming in history

Immanuel, God with us, I wonder at the truth that You are God and Man

Immanuel, God with us, I welcome Your presence here today

Immanuel, God with us, I trust in You and lean on You as I face the coming days

Immanuel, God with us, I worship You today

Amen

Consider:

1. Joseph was a real person, an ordinary man to whom something extraordinary happened. Have you allowed the 'physical world' and the 'spiritual world' to be separated in your thinking? How can you welcome the truth of Jesus into your everyday working life?
2. What difference would it make in your daily life if you leant on Immanuel, God with us?

24 Dec

Bible reading: Luke 2:1-7

For my thirtieth birthday, some of my best friends bought me two tiny antique coins. One had the head and name of Pontius Pilate on it, and the other that of Caesar Augustus. These two tiny denarii are precious to me. They are evidence from outside the Bible that the Gospel writers got details of what they were writing about correct. In our reading today we are told of the reason for Joseph and Mary travelling to Bethlehem, even though they lived in Nazareth.

We know that hundreds of years earlier, the Messiah's birth was prophesied, and was to take place in Bethlehem, but Joseph and Mary lived in another town. Again we see the hand of God in ordinary circumstances. A census is called and everyone has to return to his 'own town' – the town of his family's origin – to be counted. The whims of the bureaucracy of a superpower conspire to bring the unborn Son of God into the town where it has been predicted the Messiah would be born.

The Christmas story is not wish fulfilment. It is not a case of 'I want it to be true and so I believe in it'. Luke locates the story in the era of a specific Roman governor's particular census – we know when this happened. Luke is a doctor, a man of science, a Gentile who writes his history having thoroughly investigated his sources. History is important, and these events actually happened; Jesus' birth is not a fantasy or ethereal moral principle – it is a verifiable historical reality. God is staking a claim for our attention on Jesus of Nazareth. God is entering time, initiating relationship with us in a way that we can observe, scrutinise and make a decision about for ourselves.

But because of the upheaval of people, there was nowhere for the holy family to stay. And so the heavily pregnant Mary and her concerned husband find themselves consigned to the innkeeper's stable. Lest we get caught up in the romanticism of Christmas, this historical detail roots the story in the earthy reality of poverty, dirt and inconvenience. The time has come for the birth of Christ; all of history has been straining towards this moment. But it happens in real time amidst the physical challenges of blood, sweat and tears.

Pause to reflect:

The moment has arrived – time has been rushing towards this event, when Jesus will be born. God has arranged the prophets, planned the ancestors, chosen the mother, and now the bureaucracy of an empire to bring the details into place. Christ will be born in Bethlehem. In human history. Meditate on this and allow God's sovereignty over time to thrill you.

Pray:

Lord, let not our souls be busy inns that have no room for thee or thine,
But quiet homes of prayer and praise, where thou mayest find fit company,
Where the needful cares of life are wisely ordered and put away,
And wide, sweet spaces kept for thee; where holy thoughts pass up and down
And fervent longings watch and wait thy coming.

Julian of Norwich (1340–1426)

Consider:

1. In the anticipation of Christmas Day and amidst all the practical arrangements, how can you keep central the amazing truth of Jesus coming into the world?

25 Dec

Bible readings: Luke 2:8-14; John 1:1-5,14

The Christmas story tells us of a God who enters a sinful, suffering world. This is powerfully illustrated in Jesus' birthplace – a dirty stable. My twin boys were born in a London NHS hospital, which is not known for its sparkling cleanliness, and that was pretty traumatic, but God's Son is born into the dirt of animal refuse. The manger where He slept was the animal feeding trough.

In the location of His birth, we see that Jesus does not remain distant from the dirt and pain of our human existence. The dirtiness of the stable parallels the dirtiness of our lives – the scars we bear, the secret fears, the things we hope no one will ever find out about us. It is into this dirty world that the pure, just and perfect Son of God is born. He comes to embrace us in our real, dirty state – and to save us.

As one writer put it:

If our greatest need had been information, God would have sent us an educator;

If our greatest need had been technology, God would have sent us a scientist;

If our greatest need had been money, God would have sent us an economist;

If our greatest need had been pleasure, God would have sent us an entertainer;

But our greatest need was forgiveness, so God sent us a Savior.[5]

At the same time, the glory of the Lord shines around – the contrast with the squalor of the stable could not be greater, and the shepherds who witness it are transfixed and terrified. This is surely a natural human reaction to the appearance of a glorious angel and the very radiance and majesty of God. We are reminded of the blazing light of goodness and the love of God for a broken world.

The angels, with their grasp of time, their wonder of God and their witness of creation realise that this is a moment of great joy, of good news, and they can't keep it to themselves. They had been waiting throughout human history and now Jesus had been born – this was fantastic news for them, and they lit up the sky with their joy.

Angels are powerful spiritual beings who have been with God since the creation of the universe and the start of time. They knew something staggering when they saw it – they didn't just sing for anything and anyone! Think about what God did here – he created the universe and now He has entered into that world. As John tells us: 'Through him all things were made … The Word became flesh and made his dwelling among us' (vv.3,14).

Dr Francis Collins was the head of the human Genome project, and helped map out the DNA of humans. He is one of the most respected scientists in the world and he comments on the wonder of creation: 'When you look from the perspective of the scientist at the universe, it looks as if it knew we were coming. There are fifteen constants – the gravitational constant, various constants about the strong and the weak nuclear force … that have precise values. If any one of these constants was off by even one part in a million million, the universe would not have actually come to a point where we see it. Matter would not have been able to coalesce (join together), there would have been no galaxy, stars, plants or people.'

The One who brought the universe into existence has now been born as a baby in the very world He made. No wonder the angels rejoiced – they knew the magnitude of what had happened.

Pause to reflect:

Think about the cosmic greatness of God; now think of the fragility of a tiny newborn baby. Thank God for coming as Immanuel – God with us – at Christmas.

Pray:

Praise Him with the words of the famous carol, 'O Come, All Ye Faithful':

Yea, Lord, we greet Thee,
Born this happy morning;
Jesus to Thee be all glory given;
Word of the Father,
Now in flesh appearing!

O come let us adore Him,
O come let us adore Him,
O come let us adore Him,
Christ the Lord.

John F. Wade (1710–1786)

Consider:

1. What does it mean to you that Jesus entered into the brokenness and dysfunctionality of the real world?
2. How might His presence make a difference to you practically on this Christmas Day?

26 Dec

Bible reading: Luke 2:9-20

As you go about your daily business, at work, at school or around the home, how much do you think about God? Can you imagine what it would be like if an awesome group of shining angels turned up at your office or workplace and spoke to everyone there? The shepherds were in exactly that situation in our reading today. They were at work. The Bible doesn't mark the spiritual/ material divide as we often do. There is no biblical paradigm for sections of our lives that are somehow separate from God and His truth. There is no concept of separate 'spiritual time', and then the rest of life. God breaks into real, normal, boring time and makes Himself known. For the shepherds this was hugely surprising. God broke into time.

A glorious cohort of angels tells the shepherds of Jesus' birth – they hear that the Saviour has been born, that He is for all people and that He is Lord. The sign, or proof, of this will be that they will find the child in a manger. This detail is so familiar to us now, but it would have seemed truly odd at that time to put a baby in an animal feeding trough. If the shepherds were indeed to find the baby like this, they would know that everything they had been told about the baby's messianic status was true.

These were not elite people. Shepherding was not a well-paid or highly esteemed profession. In fact, rabbis saw shepherds as unclean and pretty low on the social scale. The shepherds would have imagined that if the child really was the Messiah, the parents would surely reject them as visitors. Hearing from the angels that the babe was lying in a manger may have reassured them that the Messiah Himself was humble and that the parents might accept them. And God chose the shepherds as the witnesses of the awesome angel choir and as the first witnesses outside of the holy family of the miracle that had happened. Immanuel, God with us, was to be first worshipped by His parents and second by a group of shepherds.

We read that after the angels left them, the shepherds hurried off to find Joseph and Mary and, when they see Jesus, He is indeed lying in a manger. The shepherds then go and tell everyone they meet about the baby, the angels and the proof and, as we might

expect, 'all who heard … were amazed' (v.18). God breaks into
the ordinary lives of working people and those same people go
on in real time and normal life to speak to others about what has
happened to them.

Pause to reflect:

Do you feel confident to tell people you meet about Jesus? Are you
familiar with the convincing evidence that He is indeed the Christ?
The shepherds knew that what they were saying was true, and so
they were confident to share with others. Think about some of
the reasons for your belief in Christ. Remind yourself of the solid
foundations of your own faith and ask the Lord to help you to speak
to others about Him.

Pray:

Thank You, Father, for the solid foundations of our faith. In the midst
of the stress and busyness of the Christmas season, I praise You
that You are the solid rock. I thank You that the basis for all of our
celebration is true and real. Help me to speak of You with clarity and
conviction. For Jesus' sake. Amen.

Consider:

1. Who can I speak to today about the real message of Christmas?
2. How can I escape some of the material trappings of Christmas and
   honour the One who lay in a manger?

27 Dec

Bible reading: Matthew 2:1-2

In our reading today we encounter a group of 'Magi'. They are learned foreigners who are star gazers, well used to deducing philosophy from the night sky and, based on what they see, they arrive in Jerusalem looking for a child who has been born King of the Jews. They have seen the evidence and, based on that, they decide to worship.

The Psalms tell us that the heavens declare the glory of God. It is not unusual for people to find their way to the Christian faith through studying cosmology and astronomy. Alister McGrath studied the stars as a teenager, and this awakened him to the possibility of God. He writes:

Back in the 1960s, we were told that religion was fading away, to be replaced by a secular world. For some of us that sounded like a great thing. I was an atheist back in the late 1960s, and remember looking forward to the demise of religion with a certain grim pleasure. I had grown up in Northern Ireland, and had known religious tension and violence at first hand ... The future was bright and godless ... I started out as an atheist, who went on to become a Christian. I had originally intended to spend my life in scientific research, but found that my discovery of Christianity led me to study its history and ideas in greater depth. I gained my doctorate in molecular biophysics while working in the Oxford laboratories of Sir George Radda, but then gave up active scientific research to study theology.[6]

But the Magi's belief deduced from the star is more specific than a belief in God. There have been many explanations as to what this star might be. Some have suggested that the Bethlehem star was a supernova, a comet, a massing of planets, or the conjunction of Jupiter and Venus on June 17, 2 BC. It could be that any of these explanations are the right one, or perhaps the star was a supernatural phenomenon placed there by God since the star Matthew describes appears to be dynamic; after all it 'went ahead of' and 'stopped over where the child was'.

The star somehow alerted the Magi to Christ's arrival, inspiring them to leave everything and travel east to Jerusalem. These Magi are generally believed to be from Persia, which is east of Jerusalem. Perhaps they knew something of the Scriptures since the prophet Daniel had lived in that region and exercised such influence in Babylonian culture. Maybe they were expecting a star to announce the birth of Christ from reading Numbers 24:17, which describes a star coming from Jacob and a King from Israel.

People often imagine that the Magi turned up at the stable the night after Jesus was born – partly because of the Nativity plays we have all seen and participated in. In fact, the Magi find Jesus living in a house (Matt. 2:11) near where He was born and this could have been up to two years later, as Herod tries to have Jesus killed and takes the precaution of killing all male children under two. The star leads these wise men to find Christ and to worship Him.

Again we reflect on God's extraordinary timing, as He leads men from far away lands using a sign in the heavens at the time of His Son's birth. He brings the high and the low, the Gentile and the Jew, the rich and the poor together to worship His Son upon His incarnation in the world.

Pause to reflect:

Reflect on the truth that the God who made the universe, including all the planets and stars, sent a star to guide seekers of truth to find His Son. The cosmic Lord who created time and matter, guides people within time using all sorts of means so that they can find Jesus and worship Him.

Pray:

Lord, may we be like the wise men who were guided to You by
a star. Give us the wisdom to seek You, light to guide us to You,
courage to search until we find You, graciousness to worship You
and generosity to lay our gifts before You, our King and our God
for ever and ever. Amen.

Consider:

1. What does it mean to you that God made the universe? Are you
   able to speak about Him as Creator?
2. Do you know people who are considered wise or influential who
   do not yet believe in Jesus? Do you believe that they are beyond
   God's revelation? Commit to pray that the wise men and women
   you know might find the Lord in the coming year.
3. Do you have any experience of God's amazing timing in your
   own life?

28 Dec

Bible reading: Matthew 2:1-8

The Magi arrive in Jerusalem, the logical destination for wise people
looking for the King of the Jews. The star had guided them from the
East and they came to a stop about six miles from Bethlehem.

The Magi are important enough to be received by Herod. Here we
learn that God in His perfect timing is able to reach the intellectual
and financial elite in any culture. When the Magi arrive at Herod's
court asking for the King of the Jews, Herod is deeply disturbed.
Already Jesus is evoking powerful emotions – some are profoundly
uncomfortable and disturbed by the prospect of Christ as King, just
as others are drawn to worship Him.

Herod assembles his learned advisors and asks them if they know where the King of the Jews was expected to be born. They are able to tell him from the prophecies of the Old Testament that the Messiah was to be born in Bethlehem. These theologians give us another insight into a recognisable reaction to Jesus Christ. They knew that Bethlehem was the town where the Messiah was to be born, they hear the miraculous testimony of these wise men, but they show no desire to go and worship. The time is now! All of their learning points to a fulfilment in Christ. But they are unable or unwilling to enter in when the time has finally come. Unlike the Magi, Herod's advisors don't want to worship. They see the truth but choose not to follow.

Sometimes we think that if only God would do some amazing miracle, people we know would finally believe. But remember – He did. But even at the time of Jesus, people saw the miracles and still chose not to follow. This should not surprise us.

The Magi want to worship, Herod's advisors do not want to worship, but King Herod is intriguing because he pretends to want to worship. He asks the Magi to go ahead and find the babe so that he too can worship Him. His words and outward actions do not reflect the state of his heart. He shows the outward signs of interest in Christ and talks about religious observance, but inside he is diametrically opposed to Christ. The Bible is not unrealistic or naïve about people, but searingly accurate about how we humans can be.

Pause to reflect:

Are you like the Magi, who wanted to worship Christ? Are you like Herod's advisors, who knew factual information about the Messiah but were not really interested in worshipping Him? Are you like Herod; are you pretending to worship Christ when actually your heart is a million miles away from submission to Him? Are you able to enter in today? The time is now! Christ has come and you can know Him now.

Pray:

Christ the light of the world has come to dispel the darkness of our hearts. In his light let us examine ourselves and confess our sins.

Silence is kept.

Lord of grace and truth,
we confess our unworthiness
to stand in your presence as your children.
We have sinned:

All **forgive and heal us.**

The Virgin Mary accepted your call
to be the mother of Jesus.
Forgive our disobedience to your will.
We have sinned:

All **forgive and heal us.**

Your Son our Saviour
was born in poverty in a manger.
Forgive our greed and rejection of your ways.
We have sinned:

All **forgive and heal us.**

The shepherds left their flocks
to go to Bethlehem.
Forgive our self-interest and lack of vision.
We have sinned:

All **forgive and heal us.**

The wise men followed the star
to find Jesus the King.
Forgive our reluctance to seek you.
We have sinned:

All **forgive and heal us.**[7]

Consider:

1. Have you ever been in the position of pretending you are worshipping when your mind and heart are miles away from God?
2. How can you be more like the Magi who got together with others who were seeking Christ and found Him together?
3. Are there things keeping you from worshipping Christ? What are they? How can you overcome these obstacles to true worship?

Group activity:

Over the last seven days, we have read about the time when the waiting was over and the Messiah finally arrived. We've looked at the responses of those at the centre of the action, including Jesus' mother Mary, the shepherds, the Magi ... God had come to be with His people. And He is with us today, by the Holy Spirit.

As a group, design a display for your church, to encourage other members and visitors with the amazing truth that we can know God's presence in our lives today. Use as a starting point the wonderful phrase 'Immanuel, God with us'. Let your worship flow in creative ways – through painting, collage, poetry. If art is not your thing, perhaps simply trace around your hand and write on it something you praise God for, evidence of His fingerprints on your life, and add this to the display.

Looking Ahead

29 Dec

Bible reading: Matthew 2:9-11

After the Magi had met with Herod, the star went on before them to Bethlehem. The star seems to have taken the Magi to the front door of the very house that Jesus was in.

When they arrive, the Magi worship with joy. We don't often associate joy with learning and wisdom. Yet these powerful, well-respected men, who had devoted their lives to intellectual pursuits, were 'overjoyed'. They were able to enter into the imminence of the moment. They grasped that something truly spectacular and wonderful was happening.

By following the star from their own country they now find it taking them to where they discover Jesus and – as amazing as it was for that culture, so it is for ours today – they bow down and worship the baby. The text is wonderful here – the joy sings out (vv.10–11). The joy of Christmas is the joy of these men – they have found the

Saviour of the world, and worshipping Him is exhilarating.

How often do you see deep and hilarious joy in your own Christian life and that of the Christian community of which you are a part? Nehemiah proclaimed, 'The joy of the LORD is your strength' (Neh. 8:10). Some of the most joy-filled Christians I have met are living in situations of great persecution, yet there is indescribable and wonderful joy in their lives, and a laughter bubbling up in conversation and fellowship. It seems to me to be pretty urgent in the West that we recapture holy joy in our churches!

How extraordinary it must have been for Mary and Joseph to hear that knock at the door – almost certainly months after Jesus' birth – and discover a bright star leading three powerful eastern men to them. The rightness of such learned people worshipping a baby speaks in itself of the nature of that baby – this is God with us. In Christ, God is entering space, time and history, taking flesh and dwelling among us.

Pause to reflect:

Meditate on the joy of those wise men; imagine the laughter and smiles of the Magi as they encounter Jesus as a baby.

Pray:

Use the majestic words of this carol to worship Christ today:

> Hail the heaven born Prince of Peace!
> Hail the Sun of Righteousness!
> Light and life to all He brings,
> Ris'n with healing in His wings.
> Mild He lays his glory by,
> Born that man no more may die.
> Born to raise the sons of earth,
> Born to give them second birth.

Hark! the herald angels sing:
'Glory to the newborn King!'

Charles Wesley (1707–1788)

Consider:

1. Is the joy of the Lord your strength?
2. Reflect on a time when you have known joy and perseverance in a dark time.
3. Are you humble enough to truly bow your knee to Christ? What might be inhibiting you?

30 Dec

Bible reading: Matthew 2:11-12

Today we read that the Magi 'opened their treasures' and presented Jesus with three significant gifts. Later in His life, Jesus would go on to teach that 'where your treasure is there your heart will be also' (Matt. 6:21), and so it is significant that these three men who have come to worship Him and pay homage to Him are prepared to open their treasure to Him. They may have given Him lots of gifts, but three are mentioned because of their significance.

The three gifts given by the Magi were gold, frankincense and myrrh. These gifts represent the roles of Jesus Christ in His relationship to us. Gold was the usual offering demanded by a king of his subjects, and it represents Jesus' royalty, rule and stature as King. It is wonderful, then, that the wise men, who are often referred to as kings, are the ones giving gold to the real King. Frankincense is incense that was used particularly in worship by priests at the

Temple, and it represents both Jesus' divine nature and the fact that He is the High Priest over all. Myrrh is one of the ingredients used in the holy anointing oil, described in Exodus chapter 30, which was set apart to consecrate the things in the Temple but more significantly was also used to embalm, anoint and deodorise the dead. The gift of myrrh to a baby is very strange, but Jesus is no ordinary child – myrrh shows us that Jesus is going to die a significant death, a representative death as a sacrifice for the sins of human beings.

The time is now – in that Jesus has come and in fulfilment of prophecy the Son of God has been born. In the gifts of the Magi we have the sense of God's perfect timing again, preparing hearts for the future. Jesus has come for a purpose and the three gifts of the wise men point forward to this eternal plan. King Jesus is the great intermediary between God and man, and He will accomplish the redemption of humanity and our reconciliation with God through His sacrificial death.

Imagine Mary's reaction to the gift of myrrh – might she be remembering at this point Simeon's warning?

Pause to reflect:

The Magi's gifts point to the ultimate gift Jesus was going to give us – His life for ours. What is an appropriate response for us today? John Piper in his sermon on this passage says:

> Gifts are intensifiers of desire for Christ himself in much the same way that fasting is. When you give a gift to Christ like this, it's a way of saying, 'The joy that I pursue (verse 10!) is not the hope of getting rich with things from you. I have not come to you for your things, but for yourself. And this desire I now intensify and demonstrate by giving up things, in the hope of enjoying you more, not things. By giving to you what you do not need, and what I might enjoy, I am saying more earnestly and more authentically, 'You are my treasure, not these things.' I think that's what it means to worship God with gifts of gold and frankincense and myrrh.[8]

Following the Magi's example – what can you give to God in worship?

Pray:

What can I give Him, poor as I am?
If I were a shepherd I would bring a lamb;
If I were a wise man, I would do my part;
Yet what I can I give Him – give my heart.

Christina Rossetti (1830–1894)

As the wise men before me, I open all my treasure to You, Jesus. Help me to give everything to You and to worship You wholeheartedly. Amen.

Consider:

1. What gifts have you given God in the past year?
2. Reflect again on the significance and meaning of the Magi's gifts.
3. Have you opened your treasure to Jesus – financial, intellectual and other?

31 Dec

Bible reading: Matthew 2:13-18

The Magi are told in a dream to go home. The God of heaven and earth speaks directly to these three in a dream and warns them about the specifics of their journey – He lets them know that they should not go home via Herod in Jerusalem. So they take an alternative route.

Next Joseph is warned in a dream to take his family to Egypt. The God of heaven and earth (the angel of the Lord) appears to Joseph in a dream and tells him to take his family across the border. Matthew shows us that again the God of all time has foreseen this and has even prophesied, 'Out of Egypt I called my son' (v.15).

Herod is enraged and has the under twos killed in a horrific episode known as the Killing of the Innocents. Such was the arrogance and desire for power of Herod that he went to extreme lengths to prevent God's will from unfolding. It is interesting that around the birth of Moses, a similar slaughter happened – the Egyptian slave masters killed the Hebrew baby boys. The arrival of grace unleashes furious and violent opposition in those who hate the Lord.

Later on, Joseph has another dream – it is now safe to return to his home. The God of heaven and earth lets Joseph know that Herod has died and he can take his family out of Eygpt. Joseph then has another dream, warning of Herod's son in Jerusalem, and so he goes to Nazareth. Again God speaks to Joseph in a dream.

We see from all this that God speaks! He speaks in a detailed and accurate way within history – guiding and warning people who trust in Him and who are involved in the events of His kingdom. He sends dreams in order to speak clearly to those who are serving Him. 'The LORD directs the steps of the godly. He delights in every detail of their lives. Though they stumble, they will never fall, for the LORD holds them by the hand' (Psa. 37:23–24, NLT). God is interested in the details of our lives, and He is able to work within time to fulfil His promises. The Magi were outsiders, foreigners, yet they were caught up in the story of redemption. It is unlikely that they knew in their lifetime the significance of the role they were playing in salvation history, prophesying the atoning death of Christ and symbolising His lordship over peoples of all nations, not just Israel, but their participation is a powerful witness to the truth that God uses ordinary people, high and low, rich and poor, men and women

– people like you and me – in His extraordinary redemptive plans for the world.

Pause to reflect:

At the dawn of a new year, ask the Lord to speak to you and guide your steps for the coming year. Take some time to write down any words or pictures He gives you.

Pray:

At the dawn of this New Year, I commit myself to You afresh. Father God, I trust You to guide my steps. I believe that You work out Your plans in our lives and I pray that in the joys and sorrows of the coming year, You will be glorified in my life. I pray that the truth of Your gospel will be proclaimed in my family, church, community and workplace. I pray that many people will turn to You and recognise You as the Redeemer of the world. In Christ's name. Amen.

Consider:

1. What do you think God is saying to you personally today as you look back on last year and look ahead to next year?
2. How can you bring the Lord into the practical details of your decision making more proactively this year?
3. Who are you hoping to speak to about Christ in this coming year? Take some time to write down the names of friends and family members who are not yet Christians, with whom you would love to be able to share your faith.

Group activity:

What has most impacted you from these Advent studies, and

how will you change as a result? Discuss this together and make some resolutions for the New Year. Pray for one another, for specific struggles and hopes, that you would each come to know and love God more, and see His purposes and timing in your lives.

Notes

1. Madeleine L'Engle, *A Wrinkle in Time*, quoted by Jill Carattini in 'Chronos and Kairos', www.rzim.org/usa/usfv/tabid/436/articleid/10349/cbmoduleid/1133/default.aspx
2. Ravi Zacharias, *The Grand Weaver* (Grand Rapids: Zondervan, 2007) pp.16–17.
3. From Michael Perry, 'See Him Lying on a Bed of Straw (Calypso Carol)'. Words © M. Perry/Administered by The Jubilate Group. St Katherines Rd, Torquay copyrightmanager@jubilate.co.uk USED BY PERMISSION
4. Collect from Common Worship: Daily are copyright © The Archbishops' Council, 2005 and are reproduced by permission.
5. Charles Sell, *Unfinished Business* (Multnomah, 1989) pp.121ff.
6. Alister McGrath and Joanna Collicutt McGrath, *The Dawkins Delusion?* (London: SPCK, 2007) pp.vii–ix.
7. Confession from *Common Worship: Services and Prayers for the Church of England* are copyright © The Archbishops' Council, 2000 and are reproduced by permission.
8. John Piper, 'We Have Come to Worship Him' (21 December 1997), http://www.desiringgod.org/resource-library/sermons/we-have-come-to-worship-him/print?lang=en

National Distributors

UK: (and countries not listed below)
CWR, Waverley Abbey House, Waverley Lane, Farnham, Surrey GU9 8EP. Tel: (01252) 784700
Outside UK (44) 1252 784700 Email: mail@cwr.org.uk

AUSTRALIA: KI Entertainment, Unit 21 317-321 Woodpark Road, Smithfield, New South Wales 2164.
Tel: 1 800 850 777 Fax: 02 9604 3699 Email: sales@kientertainment.com.au

CANADA: David C Cook Distribution Canada, PO Box 98, 55 Woodslee Avenue, Paris, Ontario
N3L 3E5. Tel: 1800 263 2664 Email: sandi.swanson@davidccook.ca

GHANA: Challenge Enterprises of Ghana, PO Box 5723, Accra. Tel: (021) 222437/223249
Fax: (021) 226227 Email: ceg@africaonline.com.gh

HONG KONG: Cross Communications Ltd, 1/F, 562A Nathan Road, Kowloon. Tel: 2780 1188
Fax: 2770 6229 Email: cross@crosshk.com

INDIA: Crystal Communications, 10-3-18/4/1, East Marredpalli, Secunderabad – 500026, Andhra
Pradesh. Tel/Fax: (040) 27737145 Email: crystal_edwj@rediffmail.com

KENYA: Keswick Books and Gifts Ltd, PO Box 10242-00400, Nairobi. Tel: (020) 2226047/312639
Email: keswick@swiftkenya.com

MALAYSIA: Canaanland, No. 25 Jalan PJU 1A/41B, NZX Commercial Centre, Ara Jaya, 47301 Petaling
Jaya, Selangor. Tel: (03) 7885 0540/1/2 Fax: (03) 7885 0545 Email: info@canaanland.com.my

Salvation Publishing & Distribution (M) Sdn Bhd, 23 Jalan SS 2/64, 47300 Petaling Jaya, Selangor.
Tel: (03) 78766411/78766797 Fax: (03) 78757066/78756360 Email: info@salvationbookcentre.com

NEW ZEALAND: KI Entertainment, Unit 21 317-321 Woodpark Road, Smithfield, New South Wales
2164, Australia. Tel: 0 800 850 777 Fax: +612 9604 3699 Email: sales@kientertainment.com.au

NIGERIA: FBFM, Helen Baugh House, 96 St Finbarr's College Road, Akoka, Lagos.
Tel: (01) 7747429/4700218/825775/827264 Email: fbfm_1@yahoo.com

PHILIPPINES: OMF Literature Inc, 776 Boni Avenue, Mandaluyong City. Tel: (02) 531 2183
Fax: (02) 531 1960 Email: gloadlaon@omflit.com

SINGAPORE: Alby Commercial Enterprises Pte Ltd, 95 Kallang Avenue #04–00, AIS Industrial Building,
339420. Tel: (65) 629 27238 Fax: (65) 629 27235 Email: marketing@alby.com.sg

SOUTH AFRICA: Struik Christian Books, Wembley Square, 1st Floor, Solan Street, Gardens, Cape Town,
8001. Tel: +27 (0) 21 460 5400 Fax: +27 (0) 21 461 7662 Email: info@struikchristianmedia.co.za

SRI LANKA: Christombu Publications (Pvt) Ltd, Bartleet House, 65 Braybrooke Place, Colombo 2.
Tel: (9411) 2421073/2447665 Email: dhanad@bartleet.com

USA: David C Cook Distribution Canada, PO Box 98, 55 Woodslee Avenue, Paris, Ontario N3L 3E5,
Canada. Tel: 1800 263 2664 Email: sandi.swanson@davidccook.ca

Courses and seminars

Publishing and new media

Conference facilities

Transforming lives

CWR's vision is to enable people to experience personal transformation through applying God's Word to their lives and relationships.

Our Bible-based training and resources help people around the world to:
• Grow in their walk with God
• Understand and apply Scripture to their lives
• Resource themselves and their church
• Develop pastoral care and counselling skills
• Train for leadership
• Strengthen relationships, marriage and family life and much more.

Our insightful writers provide daily Bible-reading notes and other resources for all ages, and our experienced course designers and presenters have gained an international reputation for excellence and effectiveness.

CWR's Training and Conference Centre in Surrey, England, provides excellent facilities in an idyllic setting – ideal for both learning and spiritual refreshment.

CWR Applying God's Word
to everyday life and relationships

CWR, Waverley Abbey House,
Waverley Lane, Farnham,
Surrey GU9 8EP, UK

Telephone: **+44 (0)1252 784700**
Email: **info@cwr.org.uk**
Website: **www.cwr.org.uk**

Registered Charity No 294387
Company Registration No 1990308

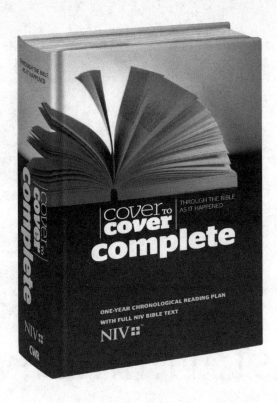

Journey through the Bible as it happened – in a year of daily readings

Read through the entire Bible in a year with 366 daily readings from *The New International Version* (NIV) arranged in chronological order.

Beautiful charts, maps, illustrations and diagrams make the biblical background vivid, timelines enable you to track your progress, and a daily commentary helps you to apply what you read to your life.

A special website also provides character studies, insightful articles, photos of archaeological sites and much more for increased understanding and insight.

Cover to Cover Complete – NIV Edition

1600 pages, hardback with ribbon marker, 140x215mm

ISBN: 978-1-85345-804-0

For current prices visit **www.cwr.org.uk/store**
Available online or from Christian bookshops